The Thirties Poets

Open Guides to Literature

Series Editor: Graham Martin (Professor of Literature,
The Open University)

Titles in the Series

W. H. Auden
(courtesy of the National Portrait Gallery)

JEM POSTER

The Thirties Poets

Open University Press
Buckingham · Philadelphia

Open University Press
Celtic Court
22 Ballmoor
Buckingham
MK18 1XW

and
1900 Frost Road, Suite 101
Bristol, PA 19007, USA

First Published 1993

A catalogue record of this book is available from the British Library

0 335 09663 8 (Paperback)   0 335 09664 6 (Hardback)

Library of Congress Cataloging-in-Publication Data
Poster, Jem.
    The thirties poets / Jem Poster.
       p.   cm.—(Open guides to literature)
    Includes bibliographical references and index.
    ISBN 0-335-09664-6.—ISBN 0-335-09663-8 (pbk.)
    1. English poetry—20th century—History and criticism.
I. Title. II. Series.
PR610.P58 1993
821'.91209—dc20   92-45681
                                                      CIP

Typeset by Best-Set Typesetter Ltd, Hong Kong
Printed in Great Britain by St Edmundsbury Press Ltd,
Bury St Edmunds, Suffolk

Contents

Series Editor's Preface

The intention of this series is to provide short introductory books about major writers, texts, and literary concepts for students of courses in Higher Education which substantially or wholly involve the study of Literature.

The series adopts a pedagogic approach and style similar to that of Open University material for Literature courses. *Open Guides* aim to inculcate the reading 'skills' which many introductory books in the field tend, mistakenly, to assume that the reader already possesses. They are, in this sense, 'teacherly' texts, planned and written in a manner which will develop in the reader the confidence to undertake further independent study of the topic. They are 'open' in two senses. First, they offer a three-way tutorial exchange between the writer of the *Guide*, the text or texts in question, and the reader. They invite readers to join in an exploratory discussion of texts, concentrating on their key aspects and on the main problems which readers, coming to the texts for the first time, are likely to encounter. The flow of a *Guide* 'discourse' is established by putting questions for the reader to follow up in a tentative and searching spirit, guided by the writer's comments, but not dominated by an over-arching and single-mindedly-pursued argument or evaluation, which itself requires to be 'read'.

Guides are also 'open' in a second sense. They assume that literary texts are 'plural', that there is no end to interpretation, and that it is for the reader to undertake the pleasurable task of discovering meaning and value in such texts. *Guides* seek to provide, in compact form, such relevant biographical, historical and cultural information as bears upon the reading of the text, and they point the reader to a selection of the best available critical discussions of it. They are not in themselves concerned to propose, or to counter, particular readings of the texts, but rather to put *Guide* readers in a position to do that for themselves. Experienced travellers learn to dispense with guides, and so it should be for readers of this series.

Graham Martin

Preface

I've used as the basis for this *Guide* Robin Skelton's Penguin anthology, *Poetry of the Thirties* (1964). Skelton's selection is substantial and wide-ranging; it gives prominence to the major figures without neglecting the minor ones, and establishes the general tendencies of the decade's poetry without obscuring its variety.

Although we shall naturally be concerned to set the poems in their wider context, our approach will demand close attention to textual detail. Discussion will be based on the assumption that you have the poems in front of you, and that you will be able to follow an argument which tends to unfold through allusion rather than extensive quotation. Like any guide, this is an adjunct to direct engagement, not a substitute for it.

I'd go further than this, recommending not simply that you have the text in front of you, but that you examine each poem carefully before reading what I have to say about it. You may find some of these poems difficult, and I understand the temptation to turn immediately to the *Guide* for an explanation; but it's important that you should establish your own view of the texts, and this becomes difficult if you rely too heavily at the outset on the perceptions of another reader. You should approach my account of each poem with an open mind but not a blank one, ready to modify your own readings in the light of my observations but never uncritically receptive of my views.

As you'll see, I've focused strongly on Skelton's anthology, but have naturally found it desirable to make occasional reference to poems not found there, as well as to prose works which help to illuminate this complex period of literary history. References for quotations from these sources are listed at the end of the *Guide* – though I haven't normally provided references for named individual poems, which you can trace easily enough in the collections of the authors concerned (see Suggestions for Further Reading). Bracketed page numbers in my text indicate the place of a poem in *Poetry of the Thirties*.

Acknowledgements

Grateful acknowledgements are due to the following:

J. M. Dent and Sons Ltd for permission to quote from the *Collected Poems* and *Collected Letters* of Dylan Thomas; Faber and Faber Ltd for poems from *The Collected Poems of Louis MacNeice*; Faber and Faber Ltd and Random House Inc. for poems from *The English Auden* and Stephen Spender's *Collected Poems 1928–1985*; David Higham Associates for the poems of Geoffrey Grigson; Oxford University Press for poems from David Gascoyne's *Collected Poems* and Bernard Spencer's *Collected Poems*; Martin Secker and Warburg Ltd for poems from Kenneth Allott's *Collected Poems*; and Sinclair-Stevenson Ltd for poems from C. Day Lewis' *Complete Poems*.

I am also grateful to Penguin Books Ltd for permission to use Robin Skelton's anthology, *Poetry of the Thirties*, as a central text.

1. Definitions

It seems sensible to begin by asking ourselves, quite simply, what we understand by the phrase 'poetry of the thirties'. Does any poem written or first published between the beginning of the decade and its end qualify for inclusion in the category? Or do we tend to use the phrase in a less literal way, excluding, for example, the work of T. S. Eliot whose 'Ash Wednesday' and 'Burnt Norton' were both published during the decade, or of W. B. Yeats, arguably at the height of his creative powers in the years leading up to his death in 1939? For most of us, the phrase will imply a particular generation of poets, the generation which, often under the influence of W. H. Auden's poetry, began to find its collective literary voice during the 1930s. The oldest of the poets represented in our survey was born in 1904, the youngest in 1916; more or less all of those commonly thought of as thirties poets were born between those two dates.

Why are we so ready to think of these poets as a generation, to group them together? Part of the answer is that the tendency to do so was present from the early years of the decade itself. In 1932 Michael Roberts, a Cambridge graduate with a strong interest in the poetry of his immediate contemporaries and a limited poetic talent of his own, edited for the Hogarth Press a slender anthology entitled *New Signatures*; among the contributors were W. H. Auden, C. Day Lewis and Stephen Spender. Roberts' preface, with its insistent generalizations about 'the writers in this book', strongly suggested a group identity; and the suggestion was reinforced by the publication of a second anthology, *New Country*, early in 1933. By June of that year, the critic Bonamy Dobrée was writing of a 'school' of poetry and describing Auden as its 'leader'.[1]

It's worth noting, however, that one of the most influential and clear-sighted of the period's literary figures publicly expressed scepticism about the very existence of such a school. Geoffrey

Grigson, whose poetry we shall be examining later and whose editorial judgement gave such distinction to the periodical *New Verse*, objected in his review of *New Country* to 'its union clamping disunion': 'What joins these writers except paper?', he asked, and went on in characteristically acerbic fashion to note that Roberts, in his preface, ' "usses" and "ours" as though he were G.O.C. a new Salvation Army or a cardinal presiding over a Propaganda'.[2] And years later Grigson returned to the point in a poem called 'Poets in Generations',[3] claiming on his own and others' behalf an 'unconformity', an inherent resistance to classification.

   Grigson's point is an important one, and we would do well to bear it in mind throughout our survey. If we uncritically lump together the poems written by an entire generation over a ten-year period we shall lose sight of their authors' individuality, as well as failing to register the extent to which particular poets developed between the beginning of the decade and its conclusion. Even so, the fact remains that there are certain tendencies and pre-occupations which seem characteristic of the decade and its litera-ture; and I believe that it's possible, through careful reading and analysis, to build up a picture which allows us to see patterns and resemblances without obscuring the 'unconformity' to which Grigson quite reasonably lays claim.

   In the opening paragraph of his pioneering study *Poets of the Thirties*, D. E. S. Maxwell described the decade as 'a plainly demarcated period with slump at its beginning and war at its end'.[4] Leaving aside my reservations about the suggestions of 'plainly demarcated', I'm interested in the way in which Maxwell, like so many commentators before and since, homes in immediately on non-literary phenomena as a means of defining the decade's poetry. I imagine that you'll be familiar with the idea that all literature is a reflection of the society which produces it and therefore needs to be set in its social context in order to be fully understood; but the poetry of the 1930s seems particularly resistant to separation from contemporary social and political developments, doubtless because those developments don't simply underlie the poems, but actually constitute, in so many cases, their primary focus. Before moving on to the detailed study of individual poets, we'll find it useful to map out some of the salient features of their social and political surroundings, perhaps keeping in view as we do so Michael Roberts' suggestion that, in the eyes of his generation at least, 'the middle-class world, the world of the nineteenth century, was definitely breaking up'.[5]

   The idea of the disintegration of past order into present chaos isn't, of course, unique to the period in which this particular generation grew up; but the degree to which notions of a lost stability and a prevailing disorder dominated the generation's thought and art is certainly remarkable. If we think for a moment about the period's history, some of the reasons for this should become clear.

The First World War was, of course, a watershed in British social and political history. 'Never such innocence again',[6] remarks Philip Larkin in a poem which brilliantly conveys the impression of a society catapulted in 1914 from an easy peace into brutal war. Such impressions are in part a matter of perspective: the urban poor of Britain or the indigenous inhabitants of her colonies would have been less likely than the nation's privileged middle and upper classes to have registered the idea of a shattered innocence. Nevertheless, the war's effect on British society in general was profound and its impact on the generation with which we're concerned, though sometimes delayed, was considerable. As Samuel Hynes points out in *The Auden Generation*, 'every memoir of the time makes clear that the First World War dominated the lives of those who were children then as much as it did the lives of their elders'.[7]

As this generation reached early adulthood, the shadow of past war was beginning to merge with the threat of a future one. John Lehmann, the editor of the 1930s periodical *New Writing* and a contributor to both *New Signatures* and *New Country*, wrote in his autobiography of the way in which a local mechanic, describing his experiences of the First World War, 'built up in my mind the picture of that blasted landscape of massacre', adding significantly: 'I tried not to believe it; I tried even harder to believe that it could not present itself again; but in my heart I knew that I was fooling myself.'[8] Recognition of the likelihood or inevitability of future conflict colours much of the poetry of the 1930s. 'What have we to look forward to?', asked Louis MacNeice in a poem published in 1934, answering his own question by gesturing towards 'a precise dawn/Of sallow and grey bricks, and newsboys crying war';[9] while in a disturbing poem published as early as 1930 Julian Bell, nephew of Virginia Woolf and a Cambridge contemporary of Lehmann, prophetically envisaged the bombing of London from the air.[10]

By the time the first bombs actually fell on London, Bell was already dead, a casualty of the Spanish Civil War. Breaking out in 1936, initially as a conflict between the Republican government and the Nationalist opposition, the war in Spain became a focus for the generation's idealistic longings for heroic action and a new social order. The ideals were unsustainable in the face of the confusion and brutality characteristic of this as of other wars; but the recurrence of the subject during our discussion of poems by W. H. Auden, Geoffrey Grigson and Stephen Spender will give you some idea of its importance in this context.

The desire for social renewal ran deep, the generation's idealistic tendencies being, as so often in such cases, inextricably bound up with a vision of contemporary decadence. It wasn't difficult, looking around Britain in the 1930s, to find evidence of society's profound sickness: 'What do you think about England', wrote Auden in *The Orators*, 'this country of ours where nobody is well?'[11] Many of the generation would have endorsed John Lehmann's suggestion that 'society is sick because it is organized on capitalist lines';[12] but to accept the diagnosis wasn't necessarily to espouse the Communist alternative. It's a point which needs emphasizing, since one of the myths which has grown up around the generation implies a widespread commitment to revolutionary socialism. Such commitment was actually comparatively rare, and as you move on to a detailed examination of the poems themselves, you'll get some sense of the hesitancy and doubt which, far more strongly than any political faith, inform the literature of the period.

In saying this, I don't want to minimize the undoubted impact of Marxist theory on this generation. Louis MacNeice described Marx and Freud as 'the figureheads of our transition';[13] and although the influence of these two thinkers may not always have been direct, it was certainly pervasive. Although both may be regarded as would-be healers, Marx of an unhealthy society and Freud of the sick mind, some aspects of their thought might well have reinforced the generation's anxieties and insecurities; and I'd like us to think about this for a moment.

There are obvious ways in which Marxist theory might seem unsettling to a generation of poets who belonged, with very few exceptions, to the privileged middle class. Marxist thought emphasizes the ascendancy of the proletariat, 'the class which holds the future in its hands';[14] the corollary to this is that, while middle-class individuals may choose to assist the proletarian struggle, the bourgeoisie itself is a doomed class which must, either voluntarily or under pressure, forfeit its privileges. Julian Bell's comment on the subject is revealing:

> I can't see how anyone with a decent intelligence can fail to see the intellectual irrefutability of the general Marxist hypothesis, and how anyone who has had the advantages of bourgeois civilization, pheasant shooting, leisure . . . and disinterestedness, can help

seeing that even the best the revolution can offer is fifth-rate by comparison.[15]

For Bell, as for others, the vision of an egalitarian society implied a disturbing element of loss.

More subtly, some of these writers are likely to have registered Marxism's insistence on the subservience of individual effort to the pressure of historical forces. It's actually an essential part of the Marxist argument that, by submitting to and moving with those forces, the individual may be able to influence history; but for many of the generation the effect of such a philosophy may well have been to reinforce a prevailing sense of helplessness, the helplessness implicit in Michael Roberts' comment, in his *New Country* preface, that the world 'is not in anybody's grip at all'. 'It is not intelligence which is lacking', he added, 'but control'.[16]

The theories of Freud also stress a lack of control, in this case over internal rather than external forces. In *The Ego and the Id* Freud speaks approvingly of the contention of his fellow psychologist, Georg Groddeck, that, far from living out the lives of our choice, 'we are "lived" by unknown and uncontrollable forces';[17] and elsewhere he takes issue with those who 'nourish the illusion of there being such a thing as psychical freedom', registering his categorical rejection of any such view.[18] Related Freudian notions of the erratically personal nature of moral and other judgements could only serve to intensify the unease of those who turned for enlightenment to this most influential of contemporary thinkers.

And even as ideological landmarks changed, the physical face of Britain was being transformed. The first forty years of this century were marked by a staggering expansion in the fields of technology and construction, and we need to bear in mind, as part of the wider context of our immediate concerns, such matters as the development of the nation's roads to accommodate the rapidly increasing numbers of motor vehicles (more than two million of them by 1930); the massive extension of the suburbs of so many British towns and cities; the large-scale building projects which created substantial urban communities in what had previously been rural areas; and the activities of the Electricity Board which between 1927 and 1936 laid down the 4000-mile grid whose pylons were the inspiration for one of Stephen Spender's most famous poems, 'The Pylons'. We shall be looking in some detail at that poem later on, raising the question of its author's response to the changing landscape he describes.

The explicit nature of Spender's references in 'The Pylons'

gives us a very clear indication of the way in which he has been influenced by a specific aspect of contemporary technology; but we should bear in mind that a writer may be influenced by his surroundings in ways which find oblique rather than direct expression in his work, and that poems which don't actually mention pylons, war, Marxism or urban poverty may nevertheless express an outlook which is in some sense conditioned by those factors. And when I talk of expressing an outlook, I'm thinking not only of what the poet says but also of the way in which he chooses to say it: as our survey unfolds, we'll be thinking about the significance of such matters as the widespread tendency to present experience in catalogue form, the recurrent fragmentation of syntax and the repetition of unanswered questions.

Such considerations bring us inevitably to the question of the relationship of these writers to the modernist movement. 'Modernism' is a notoriously slippery term, but those who have sought to define it have tended to locate the movement in Britain primarily within the first three decades of the present century. Malcolm Bradbury and James McFarlane titled their symposium *Modernism 1890–1930* (the earlier date reflecting the survey's strong emphasis on the movement's continental origins) and explained Modernism's decline around 1930 as the result of an increasing historical awareness and of a combination of social and economic factors which served to 'bring back political and economic determinism into the intellectual ideologies'.[19] There's some truth in the idea that the fundamentally aesthetic concerns of Modernism – its self-conscious emphasis on style and technique – gave ground during the 1930s to a more materialist and ethically orientated vision of the world; but we should bear in mind that this, like all such generalizations, needs to be treated with caution.

Certainly the reader of Auden's first collection, the *Poems* of 1930, is more likely to be struck by its clear affinities with Modernism than by any sense of altered perspectives. In their essay 'The Name and Nature of Modernism', Bradbury and McFarlane suggest that the modernist vision tended to 'irrationalize the rational, to defamiliarize and dehumanize the expected, to conventionalize the extraordinary and the eccentric, to define the psychopathology of *everyday* life, to intellectualize the emotional, to secularize the spiritual [and] to see ... uncertainty as the only certain thing'.[20] This seems a fair description of the early verse of Auden, a poet who during his undergraduate years had observed to Stephen Spender that 'the subject of a poem is a peg to hang the poetry on';[21] and while it's only just to add that Auden's poetry revealed, as the decade progressed, an increasing social awareness, it remains clear that neither he nor the majority of his immediate contemporaries can be neatly hived off from the modernist mainstream. It's worth emphasizing that such quarrel as the generation had with their great modernist forebears, Yeats and Eliot, had less to do with a rejection of the older poets' modernist aesthetics than with distaste for their religious and political beliefs. Eliot's movement into the Church certainly helped to make of him, as Skelton points out in the introduction to *Poetry of the Thirties*, something of a 'lost leader',[22] while there was undoubtedly something repellent to many of the poets of the 1930s in what MacNeice referred to as Yeats' 'elegant brand of fascism'.[23] Such reservations didn't, however, prevent Geoffrey Grigson from describing Yeats in 1933 as 'one of those rare creators undried and unwrinkled by time',[24] or Kenneth Allott from commenting, in a review of Eliot's *The Family Reunion* in 1939, that he was unable to 'think of a play written in English in the last fifty years which has so delighted, convinced and moved me';[25] while MacNeice introduced his 1941 study of Yeats' work with the observation that, if compiling an anthology of short poems, he would 'want to include some sixty by W. B. Yeats'. 'There is no other poet in the language,' he added, 'from whom I should choose so many'.[26]

Although I've felt it important to delineate something of the literary, social and ideological background, there's no substitute for careful examination of the poems themselves. The period is one which has been bedevilled by generalizations, generalizations which seem too often to have been a substitute for, rather than the product of, analysis of specific texts. The broad overview is desirable, but depends on detailed knowledge; and, with this point in mind, I'd like us to turn now to the first of the poets whose work forms the focus of this survey.

2. Setting the Tone: W. H. Auden

In beginning our detailed analysis with an account of the work of W. H. Auden, I may seem to be throwing you in at the deep end: Auden is undoubtedly one of the more difficult poets of his generation, with a not undeserved reputation for obscurity. He was also, however, widely regarded – again not without reason – as a leader: when Samuel Hynes entitled his study of thirties poetry *The Auden Generation*, he was simply reinforcing a view of Auden's pre-eminence which had been current since the early years of the decade itself. Although Dobrée's reference, already noted, to Auden's leadership of a 'school' of poetry needs to be treated with caution, there's no doubt that it reflects a perception already widespread by the time of the publication of *New Country* in 1933.

When Auden's contemporaries described the impact of his early work, it was often in terms of freshness, of shock; and even if it's impossible for the younger reader to appreciate fully the excitement involved, it's still clear that the publication of Auden's *Poems* in 1930 was an event of considerable cultural significance. Julian Symons, having explicitly noted that 'the shock is incommunicable', wrote of his sense, on reading *Poems*, 'of encountering something new',[1] while John Lehmann also emphasized the collection's startling freshness, observing that 'with the arrow aim of genius it exactly touched the nerve that no one had touched before'.[2] Geoffrey Grigson who, as we've already seen, could be savagely critical of spurious novelty, had no doubt of the importance of Auden's early poetry: in 1937 he devoted a double issue of *New Verse* to a survey of the poet whom he described as 'living in a new day',[3] while more than thirty-five years later he recalled the excitement of deciphering, for publication in *New*

Verse, the untidy manuscripts which constituted 'a new poetry, poems to appear again in that wonder-book, *Look, Stranger!*, in 1936'.[4]

The impact could be even more profound than these quotations imply: there's no reason to disbelieve Charles Madge's suggestion that his encounter with Auden's work dramatically changed his life. In 'Letter to the Intelligentsia', first published in *New Country*, he offers an account of his own movement from introspection to extroversion, from a state of physical and spiritual sickness to renewed health, achieved through a reading of Auden's poems. Madge's description suggests a quasi-religious conversion:

> But there waited for me in the summer morning,
> Auden, fiercely. I read, shuddered and knew
> And all the world's stationary things
> In silence moved to take up new positions.

To argue that Madge regarded Auden as a leader would seem, in the circumstances, something of an understatement.

Auden was himself very much interested in the idea of leadership. Stephen Spender's account of his life at Oxford in the late 1920s emphasizes the older poet's acute sense of his own potential as a leader:

> He thought that the literary scene in general offered an empty stage. 'Evidently they are waiting for Someone', he said with the air of anticipating that he would soon take the centre of it. However, he did not think of himself as the only writer of the future ... A group of emergent artists existed in his mind, like a cabinet in the mind of a party leader.[5]

Whether or not it reflects the weight actually given to the word by Auden, Spender's capitalization of 'Someone' is suggestive of something more than a merely literary leadership, while the political analogy is undoubtedly significant; Madge's response to Auden's poems may appear excessive, but he was by no means the only member of his generation to interpret the literary developments of the early 1930s as a form of spiritual and political awakening, or to link this idea with notions of the guidance and support of a strong leader.

Auden's own preoccupation with the concept of leadership is clearly reflected in his poetry: emblematic figures such as 'the tall unwounded leader' ('From scars where kestrels hover') and the godlike 'political orator' ('The chimneys are smoking') jostle with the demagogues of the age: 'Hitler and Mussolini in their wooing poses/Churchill acknowledging the voters' greeting/Roosevelt at the microphone' ('Easily, my, dear you move'). 'Who will save?'

asks the poet in an ode dedicated to the son of his friend Rex
Warner, 'Who will teach us how to behave?' ('Ode IV', *The
Orators*). The general tone of the ode may suggest a certain levity,
but the questions themselves are far from frivolous.

I'd like you to bear these points in mind as we move on to
examine one of Auden's earliest published poems, 'Sir, no man's
enemy' (p. 201). Who is the 'Sir' of the poem's opening line?
There's no simple answer to this question, but the appeal to
a figure of authority is unmistakable; you might, moreover,
remember that Gerard Manley Hopkins, a poet whose influence is
apparent in the diction of a number of Auden's early poems,
addresses God as 'sir' in his sonnet 'Thou art indeed just'; and it's
clearly not inappropriate to interpret Auden's poem as a kind of
prayer, a plea for the benevolent intervention of a higher power.
Please now read the poem.

DISCUSSION

That this is a difficult poem is apparent from the outset. What do
you make of the first two lines? Interpretation becomes easier in
the light of Auden's later apology for their obscurity: 'I bitterly
regret', he wrote on a friend's copy, 'the day I was snobbish
enough to use an archaic genitive (= will's)'.[6] Armed with this
information, and recognizing that 'be prodigal' is an injunction or
entreaty, you should now be able to make sense of the syntax, but
might still be left wondering what Auden means by 'will's negative
inversion'. Again we may be helped by looking beyond the text
itself: this is a poem deeply informed by the theories of Homer
Lane, an American psychologist to whose work Auden had been
introduced by a Berlin acquaintance, John Layard, in 1928. Lane's
view that sickness was the result of inhibited desire clearly underlies the phrase 'the distortions of ingrown virginity'; and I think
we can understand the 'negative inversion' of the will in a
similar way, as signifying energies which, instead of being allowed
expression, are turned back on themselves; such repression, Auden
suggests here, constitutes the only unforgiveable sin.

Lane argued not merely that repression bred sickness, but
that the particular form in which the sickness manifested itself was
appropriate to the nature of the repression; hence the reference to
the 'liar's quinsy', an inflammation of that area of the body most
directly implicated in the refusal to speak honestly. In his essentially
autobiographical 'novel', *Lions and Shadows*, Christopher Isherwood describes how his own explanation of his tonsilitis as the
result of a chill was countered by 'Weston's' (Auden's) blunt

assertion: 'It means you've been telling lies.'[7] Those who live unskilfully require treatment; and Auden appeals to his unspecified authority figure to establish a schoolmasterly discipline, prohibiting those responses which lack spontaneity, correcting the 'stance' (in the context of Lane's theories the term implies both physical bearing and mental attitude) of those whose courage is inadequate to the demands of life. Those who seek to escape those demands should be exposed to scrutiny: 'spotted' suggests that they have been picked out by spotlights, by the 'beams' of the preceding line, which themselves refer back to the request for 'power and light' and forward to the 'shining' of the poem's penultimate line; but you might like to consider the possibility that the would-be escapers are also 'spotted' in the sense of being marked by their diseases. You may feel that you have to opt for one or other of these interpretations, and I certainly give greater weight to the former in my own reading of the poem; but it's possible to accommodate both, to set up a fruitful interplay between the images involved, and you might find it generally helpful to your studies to think about this for a moment.

Your sense of this poem as a prayer addressed to a divine authority may be heightened by its conclusion. To harrow is to disturb, and in an agricultural context the term refers to the breaking up of ground prior to the sowing of seed – an idea appropriate enough in a poem fundamentally concerned with physical and spiritual regeneration. But the dominant suggestion here is of Christ's harrowing of Hell, the redemption, as described in the apocryphal gospel of Nicodemus, of souls previously excluded from heaven by the sin of Adam. The assault on the 'house of the dead' is the prelude to the construction of a vital, and perhaps even by implication heavenly, new world. Auden's subsequent rejection of this poem on the grounds that 'I have never liked modern architecture'[8] seems, in its absurd literalism, to betray the visionary impulse which so clearly informs it.

I suggested that this was a difficult poem, and it may be helpful at this stage to consider further a quality particularly evident in Auden's early work and characterized by Dylan Thomas as 'careful obscurity'.[9] Why might a poet actively choose (as Thomas' well-judged phrase suggests) to write in an obscure way? If part of the answer is that Auden enjoyed playing the role of *enfant terrible*, flouting literary and linguistic convention even as he challenged standard patterns of social behaviour, this needn't imply a lack of purpose. Was it really snobbery which was responsible for the archaic genitive in the first line of 'Sir, no man's enemy', or was it Auden's intention to jolt the

reader's expectations by confronting him or her with the syntactically unfamiliar? We can't of course provide definitive answers
to questions of authorial intent, but it might be instructive to look
briefly at a passage from 'It was Easter as I walked in the public
gardens', a poem written in the same year as 'Sir, no man's enemy'
and marked by a comparable but far more sustained assault on
conventional syntax:

> Is first baby, warm in mother,
> Before born and is still mother,
> Time passes and now is other
> Is knowledge in him now of other,
> Cries in cold air, himself no friend.
> In grown man also, may see in face
> In his day-thinking and in his night-thinking
> Is wareness and is fear of other,
> Alone in flesh, himself no friend.

It's not my purpose here to tease out the meaning (or
meanings) of this staccato account of human alienation, but I do
want to suggest that the disruption is deliberate, and that its effect
may be positive: by refusing us refuge in familiar structures, Auden
is making us respond freshly to the language and, arguably, to the
ideas embodied in it.

Syntactical disruption of this kind isn't the only source of
obscurity; that lack of specificity which we've touched on in our
examination of 'Sir, no man's enemy' is a recurrent and in some
respects disturbing feature of Auden's work, in particular of the
early poems. How do we respond to a poem which begins 'Nor
was that final...', leaving us completely ignorant as to what
'that' might be? Or to these lines, which open another of the
enigmatic offerings in his first collection?

> Suppose they met, the inevitable procedure
> Of hand to nape would drown the staling cry
> Of cuckoos...

As you attempt to picture this encounter, you'll inevitably register
the indistinctness of Auden's own sketch, the equivocal nature of
its outlines. Who are 'they'? Auden doesn't even define their
gender, let alone their character and appearance. Whose hand is
on whose nape? We may visualize two figures standing apart from
one another, one or both holding a hand to his/her/their own
nape(s), or may interpret the gesture quite differently, as the
embrace of the two as they kiss. Similar uncertainties are likely to
inform your reading of 'We made all possible preparations'
(p. 86), a poem which, with its austere diction and apparent

emotional detachment, reads rather like an official report. But what is the subject of the report? And who is the speaker?

To say that we can't answer such questions with any exactitude isn't a matter of evasion, but of respect for the nature of a poem which relies for its effect on a suggestive imprecision. A phrase such as 'all the orders expedient/In this kind of case' derives much of its chilling impact from the very vagueness which precludes a specific interpretation. We can map the broad outlines of the situation: a more or less overtly oppressive regime, its own future apparently bleak, asserts its authority over a populace which may protest or even on occasion offer physical resistance, but which ultimately capitulates to the demands of its rulers. But to locate and define its details much more precisely than this would be to violate the spirit of a poem which, while undoubtedly responsive to the darkening political scene in contemporary Europe and beyond, offers a vision of calculating tyranny which clearly transcends its immediate historical context.

In acknowledging, as I think we must, that the identity of the speaker remains vague throughout, we're also implying that the voice is not, in any simple sense, that of the poet himself. Other poems written by Auden at about the same time suggest a similar dislocation between poet and speaker: 'Having abdicated with comparative ease' is a good example, as is 'Since you are going to begin to-day'. It's worth noting that the title which Auden subsequently gave to the latter poem, 'Venus Will Now Say a Few Words', is one which pointedly insists on that dislocation.

Where the voice isn't simply or clearly that of the poet, how do we respond to the views or attitudes expressed? The question is of central importance to our reading of 'A Communist to Others' (p. 54), a poem which, on its appearance in *New Country* in 1933, was doubtless interpreted by many readers as a more or less direct statement of Auden's own political beliefs. Yet the title itself seems to effect a subtle dissociation of a kind which might have aroused the suspicions of the more perceptive of his contemporary readers, while modern commentators have generally avoided identifying the speaker with Auden himself. 'The voice of this poem,' argues Edward Mendelson in his 1981 study, 'is not Auden's, but that of a Communist telling Auden what he needs to learn'.[10] Please now read the poem.

DISCUSSION

Although Mendelson's statement functions as a useful corrective to any simplistic view of the poem as a personal manifesto, it might strike you as being itself a little too clear-cut. Mendelson himself goes on to register a tension between the communist's supposed proletarian background and his familiarity with the 'intellectual fashions of the bourgeoisie – mysticism, psycho-analysis, Cambridge liberalism'[11] while, more recently, Valentine Cunningham has noted the 'prep-school rhetoric' of the phrase 'Ah, what a little squirt is there.'[12] Cunningham explicitly charac-terizes that rhetoric as 'Audenesque'; both the preoccupations and the diction of the speaker suggest that, while he can't be straight-forwardly identified with the poet, neither can he be cleanly dissociated from him.

Do you find this uncertainty disturbing? I think this is likely to be the case, but you may also find it, as I do, revealing. Confusion of identity or of allegiance isn't a merely accidental feature of Auden's early poetry, but a central concern. It might prove instructive in this connection to dip into his offbeat 'English Study', *The Orators*, especially the section entitled 'Journal of an Airman', with its sinister suggestions of conflict between opposing forces whose very nature is largely unclear. The journal's repeated warnings and instructions presuppose an enemy capable of merging with its opposition; and ideas of espionage and betrayal, implying the confusion, through interpenetration, of the enemy with one's own party, contribute significantly to the characteristic mood and tone of Auden's early writings in general. We can't say with any precision how far these features reflect the poet's own moral confusions and uncertainties, but you might like to consider the implications of Auden's retrospective observation that his own name on the title page of *The Orators* seemed to be 'a pseudonym for someone else, someone talented but near the border of sanity, who might well, in a year or two, become a Nazi'.[13]

You may have noticed too that the 'you' of 'A Communist to Others' isn't fixed, but shifts from one focal point to another as the poem proceeds. The 'Comrades' of the first stanza, for example, pouring from 'office shop and factory' are clearly not to be identified with the 'splendid person', representative of privilege and affluence, in the fifth. We don't need to regard these shifts as further evidence of confusion (we'll arrive at a satisfactory reading by imagining the speaker rounding now on one representative of the doomed system, now on another) but they do suggest a com-plexity unacknowledged by Mendelson's assertion that the speaker is 'telling Auden what he needs to learn'. In addition to the degraded workers and the 'splendid person', his audience includes the mystic whose 'goodness game' is defined as evasive cowardice, the 'wise man' comfortably insulated from the misery upon which he pontificates, and a poet whose loneliness and escapism seem to suggest a generic significance rather than direct self-reference on Auden's part.

In view of the scathing references to mysticism, you may be surprised by the poem's conclusion, with its celebration of the invisible bonds created by a love 'outside our own election' – that is, a love which transcends the individual will. Mendelson points out that this conclusion is indebted to Gerald Heard's *Social Substance of Religion*, and even without this information we're likely to sense that the impulse behind the poem's closing lines is a fundamentally religious one, comparable to that which informs 'Sir, no man's enemy' and arguably at odds with the materialist doctrines of Marxism. It's as though the poet himself, having for so long remained half-concealed behind the persona of his hypothetical communist, has finally stepped out into the open.

Auden was in fact much preoccupied throughout the 1930s with the idea of love as a means of radical social transformation. In 'To a Writer on His Birthday' (p. 167), he reminds the writer in question, Christopher Isherwood, of an earlier vision of love's redemptive power:

> Surely one fearless kiss would cure
> The million fevers, a stroking brush
> The insensitive refuse from the burning core.
> Was there a dragon who had closed the works
> While the starved city fed it with the Jews?
> Then love would tame it with his trainer's look.

If, looking back over a gap of four years, Auden seems to hint at the naivety of the vision, this clearly doesn't imply total rejection. His 1939 formulation, in a poem we shall be going on to examine later, is tougher, altogether more sombre, yet reflects the same fundamental concern: 'We must love one another or die' ('September 1, 1939').

Let's look more closely at 'To a Writer on His Birthday', a poem which seems to me, in its combination of poise and audacity, characteristic of Auden at his best; as you read it, look out for meanings beneath the brilliant surface of the opening stanzas. The 'islands' of the first line offer a useful point of entry: if, while acknowledging their actuality, we appreciate that they also have a broadly metaphorical significance, we shall begin to register the poem's deeper resonances.

DISCUSSION

You'll no doubt remember the 'unhappy poet' of 'A Communist to Others', fleeing to 'islands in [his] private seas'; the injunction to 'return' implies an attitude to insularity which is also reflected in a poem written in the following year, 'Hearing of harvests rotting in the valleys', where we find a vision of a regenerate world in which 'we rebuild our cities, not dream of islands'. Dreaming and insularity are similarly closely associated in 'To a Writer on His Birthday': the holidaymakers are described as living 'their dreams of freedom'. I think you'll see at once that the suggestion is of an illusory state very different from true freedom; but the skill and subtlety with which Auden insists on this point demand more detailed analysis.

At the heart of this poem lies the tension between the illusion of control and the fact of subservience to uncontrollable forces. The statement that the holiday crowds 'control/The complicated apparatus of amusement' has been compromised before it is made. These are, after all, only 'dreams', dreams whose absurdity expresses itself in the dreamers' assumptions of their own import- ance; the suggestion of the gulls' eager attentiveness plainly invites ridicule. You may, moreover, have noticed the counter-suggestions of the first stanza, in which the holiday-makers are described as 'caught by waiting coaches, or laid bare/Beside the undis- criminating sea'. We normally speak of catching our transport rather than being caught by it; Auden's inversion implies the trippers' helpless submission, while 'laid bare' suggests a similar, and decidedly disturbing, passivity on the part of the sunbathers. The 'undiscriminating sea' is clearly relatable to the 'dangerous flood/Of history' of the final stanza, an impersonal force which sweeps men onward regardless of any attempted containment, and renders 'impossible' the 'beautiful loneliness of the banks' – that is, the insular existence additionally represented by the 'frozen plains' as well as by the 'academy and garden' of the eleventh stanza.

Auden had perhaps less confidence than many of his con- temporaries in the efficacy of literature as an agent of social change: 'poetry makes nothing happen', he insisted in his 1939 elegy, 'In Memory of W. B. Yeats'. Such redemptive possibilities as are offered by this poem are certainly rooted in a vision of literature's corrective powers (it is the 'strict' pen of Isherwood which will counter the 'flabby' fancies detailed in the earlier part of the poem, as well as providing 'nearer insight to resist/The expanding fear, the savaging disaster') but this doesn't imply any simple or narrow view of literature's social function. The significance of Auden's desire for writing which makes 'action urgent and its nature clear' can perhaps be more fully appreciated when the stanza in which it appears is set beside a passage from his introduction to *The Poet's Tongue*, an anthology published shortly before he wrote his birthday tribute to Isherwood:

> Poetry is not concerned with telling people what to do, but with extending our knowledge of good and evil, perhaps making the necessity for action more urgent and its nature more clear, but only leading us to the point where it is possible to make a rational and moral choice.[14]

In tightening up the central phrase for use in his poem, Auden gave it a more assertive cast, but I don't feel that the changes imply any significant deviation from his original suggestion that literature is a means of illuminating possibilities rather than a specific recipe for direct action.

Please now read 'Spain' (p. 133), and consider whether it accords with this view of literature. One modern critic has described it as 'a propaganda poem';[15] does this phrase seem appropriate? As we go on to examine the poem in detail, you may be struck by a certain reserve or distance; does it surprise you to learn that Auden had actually been in Spain immediately before writing it?

DISCUSSION

The sense of distance is apparent from the outset. The poem may indeed be concerned with contemporary Spanish politics, but Auden chooses to approach his subject by way of a long historical perspective which, explicitly acknowledging 'all the past', highlights such features as the dissemination of calculating skills, the invention of machinery, the impact of navigation and the manifestations of religious belief. The breadth of vision which accommodates this range of historical process also comprehends the geographical immensities implicit in the reference to the trade routes linking Europe and China; you may be reminded by this, or by the later reference to Spain as 'that arid square,/That fragment nipped off from hot/Africa . . . that tableland scored by rivers', of the opening lines of 'Consider this and in our time', in which Auden recommends the godlike perspective of 'the hawk . . . or the helmeted airman'. It's a perspective which he clearly found imaginatively liberating, but which may be taken to imply a degree of detachment from the objects of his scrutiny.

You'll notice how the incantatory 'Yesterday . . . Yesterday' is counterpointed in the fourth stanza and beyond by the recurring phrase 'But to-day the struggle'. If the manifestations of 'yesterday' suggest breadth and diversity, this phrase seems to insist, with stubborn monotony, on the circumscribed brutality of the present. And when Auden enlarges upon the phrase in the antepenultimate and penultimate stanzas, the negative suggestions remain: 'today' is marked by the sense of guilt at what he terms 'the necessary murder', by the dullness of political meetings and pamphleteering, by 'makeshift consolations' and the embrace which may be intended to express love but which prefaces the infliction of pain. Commenting on the first of these two stanzas, George Orwell described it as

> a sort of thumbnail sketch of a day in the life of a 'good party man'. In the morning a couple of political murders, a ten-minutes' interlude to stifle 'bourgeois' remorse, and then a hurried luncheon and a busy afternoon and evening chalking walls and distributing leaflets. All very edifying.[16]

How, in the light of your reading of the poem as a whole, do you respond to Orwell's account? I think you'll see at once that it's a crude travesty, and one which fails to give due weight to Auden's implied distaste for the affairs he describes. 'Today' must, he suggests, be faced if there is to be a worthwhile future; but the confrontation seems to be envisaged without pleasure.

'Tomorrow', on the other hand, is defined in positive terms. The inhibiting weight of the reiterated 'But to-day the struggle' is countered by an outward impulse, by images of richness and enlargement comparable to those associated with the past in the poem's opening stanzas: tomorrow offers 'the gradual exploring of all the/Octaves of radiation . . . the enlarging of consciousness' as well as lakeside walks and the exhilarating speed of cycle-racing. You may have noticed the directness with which Auden contrasts present and future: the solitary, whispering poet of the seventh stanza gives place to the 'young poets exploding like bombs', grouped, strongly audible and dynamically outward-moving, in the twenty-third; the 'rediscovery of romantic love' provides a desirable alternative to 'the/Fumbled and unsatisfactory embrace'; and the 'scraping concert' finds its positive counterpart in the expansive and beautiful 'roar of the chorus under the dome'.

The vision of the future is an attractive one, but Auden's attitude is guarded, uncertain: 'To-morrow, perhaps the future' is the phrase with which he introduces his series of projections; the suggestion isn't simply that the particular future he envisages may not materialize, but that mankind may have no future at all. And whatever force we allow to the images of a new life, we can't fail to register the counter-pressure of the powerful final stanza, with its references to lifelessness, isolation and defeat. The natural universe is indifferent to man's plight, while the forces of history will not intervene on his behalf; the implied argument is perhaps that we should therefore take our future into our own hands, but any suggestion of a call to action is radically subverted by the stanza's profound and resonant pessimism. Returning to the questions with which I introduced our discussion, you may find yourself quite simply disinclined to read 'Spain' as a 'propaganda poem', in which role it would seem largely ineffectual. I believe that the poem is, rather, one in which Auden seeks to 'make action urgent' and its nature as clear as the difficult circumstances allow. Judged on this basis, it seems to me an impressive piece of work, a lucid and imaginative portrayal of the hopes and fears of a generation acutely aware of the broad political and moral significance of the Spanish Civil War.

'Spain' is a public poem, large-scale and patently rhetorical. As we turn now to a poem of a far more intimate nature, it may be worth reflecting on the sheer variety of Auden's work, its resistance to categorization: 'Lay Your Sleeping Head' (p. 191) was written only a few weeks earlier than 'Spain', yet differs dramatically from it in terms both of tone and content.

DISCUSSION

The opening line defines the poem as an address to a lover, and its immediate context as the privacy of the bedroom. As we read on, we become aware of a wider and more threatening environment, as well as of the operation of Auden's analytical mind upon the experience itself; but this remains an intensely personal work.

The vulnerability of the enclosed space occupied by the lovers becomes apparent almost at once. The adjectives 'human' and 'faithless', one applied to the sleeper, the other to the speaker, both hint at impermanence, and the four succeeding lines enlarge upon the theme: the 'child' is subject to the ravages of age and sickness, and ultimately to the power of death. In spite of this recognition, however, the enclosure has not been fully breached: within the circle of the speaker's arms, the sleeper can at least rest 'till break of day'. His mortality and guilt (not merely, I think, his own personal guilt, but his inheritance of original sin) are acknowledged, yet he remains, in the eyes of his lover, somehow inviolate, 'entirely beautiful' despite the destructive forces ranged against both wholeness and beauty.

How do you understand the first line of the rather difficult second stanza? 'Soul and body have no bounds' is an ambiguous statement which might be taken to mean simply that both are capable of unlimited outward movement; I think you'll agree, however, that the suggestion here is of a lack of division between the two. Lovers and mystics may seem to differ fundamentally from one another in their respective approaches to experience, the former apparently seeking physical sensation and the latter spiritual insight; yet, Auden argues, the bodily union of the lovers is attended by a divinely instigated vision of their own relationship to the supernatural, while the hermit's stringent self-denial produces an ecstasy resembling that of the lovers in its sensuality.

The stroke of midnight is the time at which magic proverbially loses its efficacy, and the suggestion here is of a fairytale world encroached upon by a reality at once tedious and threatening. It's important to recognize that 'not a whisper . . . be lost' isn't a structure suggestive of future certainties but a subjunctive usage with the force of an entreaty; this paves the way for the final stanza's prayer for prolongation of the sustaining powers vouchsafed to the couple by their night of love. You'll perhaps be struck by the unselfishness with which the speaker requests this gift on behalf of the sleeper; elegantly poised, characteristically analytical, this is nevertheless a love poem of considerable tenderness and emotional power.

Equally powerful, though in a very different way, is 'Ballad' (p. 259). Even without the assistance of the title, I think you'd have been aware of this poem's debt to the folk tradition: the simple but highly charged language and the insistent verbal patterns and repetitions are indicative of the kind of interest which also informed Auden's choice of verse for *The Poet's Tongue*: 'I know of no other anthology,' wrote Montagu Slater in a perceptive review, 'with such a preponderance of anonymous folk poetry'.[17] Auden's interest resulted in a number of poems clearly indebted to folk sources (you might like to look at 'Johnny', 'As I Walked Out One Evening' or the trio of narrative poems, 'Miss Gee', 'Victor' and 'James Honeyman') but he never, I think, used these sources to greater effect than in 'Ballad'.

DISCUSSION

The situation defined by the dialogue – the edgy questions and the placatory but deeply suspect responses – is in one sense clear enough: a group of soldiers is approaching a couple, one of whom, in an act of apparent betrayal, abandons the other to his fate. But you'll be aware, once again, of the lack of specificity we've noted in other, rather different poems. Who are the protagonists? Who are the soldiers? And for what crime or allegiance is one of the former being hunted down, as it appears, by the latter? You may be tempted to look for clues – the scarlet uniforms, for example, which suggest a reasonably remote historical period – but you won't get very far along these lines. Nor, I would suggest, do you need to: Auden himself, with another poem in mind, made a statement which seems apposite to the present case:

> It is quite unimportant, though it is the kind of question not infrequently asked, who the soldier is, what regiment he belongs to, what war he had been fighting in, etc. The soldier is you or me, or the man next door. Only when it throws light on our own experience . . . does poetry convince us of its significance.[18]

What Auden does in 'Ballad' is to take the reader down to those levels of archetypal experience which are more or less universally meaningful. By bleaching out individualizing detail, he achieves a potent breadth of reference; this is an account of doom, terror and betrayal, shedding its light equally on private nightmare and contemporary political reality.

It seems appropriate to conclude our survey of Auden's work by examining a poem with a strongly valedictory flavour, 'September 1, 1939'. In January 1939, Auden, together with Isherwood, had left Britain and gone to live in the United States, a move interpreted by some as an act of cowardice or evasion. 'September 1, 1939' may have been written from a position of relative safety, but it's certainly not an evasive poem; at once personal and globally aware, it actually suggests a remarkably direct confrontation of contemporary events and the emotions generated by them.

September 1, 1939 was the date of the German invasion of Poland, the event which precipitated Britain's declaration of war two days later. Three months short of the decade's close, Auden contemplates the expiry of its 'clever hopes'; the phrase seems applicable on a personal as well as a more broadly social level, evidence perhaps of the maturing writer's dissatisfaction with his own poetic achievement to date, as well as an acknowledgement of the delusive vanity of a generation's longings for a new world.

DISCUSSION

I hope you noticed the familiar suggestions of a godlike perspective: the vision of waves of emotion circulating over the 'bright/And darkened lands of the earth' implies an elevated vantage point. But you'll see too that Auden isn't dissociating himself from the emotion: the poem's third line has already defined him as 'uncertain and afraid', and he now goes on to represent anger and fear as 'obsessing our private lives'. The pronoun itself is indicative of a new breadth of sympathy; this is 'our world', a world in which 'we must suffer', in which 'we must love one another or die'.

The 'whole offence' which might be uncovered by scholarly research is that which has brought the world to its present state. It's possible to read the phrase 'From Luther until now' as comprehending only the history of Germanic culture, but there's a plausible case for a wider reading: John Fuller has drawn attention to a relevant passage in the preface to Auden's *Poets of the English Language*, published thirteen years later, in which Auden blames Luther, Machiavelli and Descartes for the dualism which separates 'the individual from society, feeling from intellect and conscience from both'.[19] The reference to Linz, the town in which Hitler spent part of his early life, is more specific: just as the historian can explain the development of a culture, so analysis can expose the sources of a tyrant's mental disturbance. 'Imago' is a term used in psychology to denote the image which one individual projects onto another, usually in the context of a parent-child relationship. Auden may be suggesting that Hitler's image of his father became, in his own mind, that of a 'psychopathic god' or, alternatively, that the dictator owes his status to the projections of his followers. 'Accurate scholarship' is perhaps, however, unnecessary: the simple truth, apparent even to a child, is that evil begets evil.

And the pattern, Auden goes on to suggest in the following stanza, is recurrent. Thucydides, whose exile on a charge of military incompetence may have had particular significance for Auden as he contemplated his own position, was the author of the *History of the Peloponnesian War*, a chronicle which unfolds partly through its author's reportage of the protagonists' political and military speeches. Auden may have been thinking particularly of Cleon, a man 'remarkable among the Athenians for the violence of his character', whose savage contribution to the Mytilenian debate began, according to Thucydides, with a dismissal of democracy as 'incapable of governing others'.[20] The concluding line of the stanza seems to refer directly to Thucydides' own statement, in the introduction to his *History*, that his words are intended for those 'who want to understand clearly the events which happened in the past and which (human nature being what it is) will, at some time or other and in much the same ways, be repeated in the future'.[21]

The stigmatization of political rhetoric as 'rubbish' finds echoes in the sixth stanza, in which the words of 'Important Persons' are characterized as 'militant trash'. It's doubtless with the politicians' debased and windy verbiage in mind that Auden raises, towards the end of the poem, the possibility of an alternative voice, one which might penetrate the isolation of the deaf and articulate the experience of the dumb; and it's his own voice, with its limited but by no means negligible powers, which is offered in the poem's penultimate stanza. You'll perhaps have noticed the resemblance between the ideas expressed here and those discussed earlier in connection with 'To a Writer on His Birthday'; again we find the concept of a stringent assault on falsehood leading to a vision of austere truths. The poem's concluding stanza confronts 'the night', the darkness unacknowledged by those evasive masses for whom 'The lights must never go out'. Yet the closing lines suggest a tentative hope: 'negation and despair' may predominate, but recognition of the 'ironic points of light', of those virtues which may not be able to dispel the darkness but can at least alleviate it, brings the poem to rest on a cautiously affirmative note.

Auden's dismissal of 'a low dishonest decade' was subsequently echoed by his repudiation of the poem itself as 'infected with an incurable dishonesty'[22] or, still more sweepingly, as 'the most dishonest poem I have ever written'.[23] He himself located its dishonesty in the first instance in the line 'We must love one another or die', though his objection, that 'we must die anyway', seems to give the original statement an unnecessarily literal slant. You might like to consider Mendelson's argument that Auden was actually troubled by his representation of love as 'hunger', as mere necessity;[24] and you might also take account of the fact that both the title and form of the poem recall W. B. Yeats' 'Easter 1916', bearing in mind Auden's later claim that Yeats seduced him into 'writing poems which were false to my personal and poetic nature'.[25]

You'll readily appreciate the point that Auden's subsequent commitment to Christianity would have rendered unpalatable some of the views expressed in this as in other poems written during the 1930s; but you might usefully ask yourself whether this necessarily implies dishonesty at the time of writing. Again, the influence of Yeats is clear enough; but is it so strong or disruptive as to invalidate the poem? My own feeling is that 'September 1, 1939', while undoubtedly flawed, is rich with resonances of a kind not normally associated either with dishonest discourse or with mere pastiche. Like 'Spain', it seems to me an important poem, consolidating Auden's reputation as spokesman for a troubled generation in a difficult age.

3. A Window on the World: Stephen Spender

I noted in my opening chapter that the early years of the twentieth century saw massive expansion in the fields of technology and construction; and if we're looking for an explanation for the recurrence, in the poetry of the 1930s, of images suggestive of a creative interest in recent technological developments, we might be satisfied with the idea that the poets in question were simply registering the details of their actual environment. The matter is in fact rather more complex than this: this was indeed a poetic generation acutely conscious of its physical surroundings, but it was also a highly literate generation, and many of its members would have been aware of recent attempts to formulate an aesthetic which would give a prominent place to the manifestations of an increasingly sophisticated technology.

You may have come across the term 'Futurism', used to denote a movement which, under the energetic leadership of the Italian Filippo Tomasso Marinetti, became widely influential in the years immediately preceding the outbreak of the First World War. Marinetti and his followers exalted the idea of mechanical beauty, suggesting that the modern artist should focus on the clean lines and rhythms of the machine. There was considerable interest in Futurist ideas in England: Vorticism, an English movement which to some extent dissociated itself from Italian Futurism, was nevertheless influenced by it; and, whatever the source, the

idea of an art informed by the mechanical was much in the air at
the time. T. E. Hulme, whose theories played a part in establishing
the framework both of Vorticism and of the contemporary poetic
movement known as Imagism, spoke with enthusiasm, in an essay
written in 1914, of a new art in which the 'use of mechanical
lines' (he was thinking of the visual arts) reflected not merely an
altered environment but a radical 'change of sensibility'.[1]

The assimilation of modern technology into contemporary art
was clearly still an issue long after the heyday of the Futurist and
Vorticist movements. I mentioned earlier the two anthologies,
New Signatures and *New Country*, regarded by their editor,
Michael Roberts, as representative of his generation's concerns. As
well as Spender's 'The Express', which we shall be examining in
detail later, the first of the two anthologies included an admittedly
ironic poem by John Lehmann entitled 'This Excellent Machine'
and a verbal sketch by A. S. J. Tessimond entitled 'La Marche des
Machines'; while the second included Richard Goodman's 'The
Squadrons' (an idealization of the power of military aircraft) and
Tessimond's 'Steel April', with its celebration of 'the lovely world/Of
wavesmooth tyrannous cars and departures in the Golden Arrow'.

The generic term 'pylon poets', current during the decade
itself, must, like all popular tags, be treated with caution; but it's
clearly not inappropriate to suggest that many of the poets of the
period were actively exploring the imagistic potential of a rapidly
developing technology. Though this was only one aspect of his
varied work, Stephen Spender might justifiably be regarded as the
archetypal 'pylon poet': one of the most striking of the poems in
his first collection was simply entitled 'The Pylons', and other
poems in the same volume focus similarly sharply on the machinery
and structures of the modern world. Please now read 'The Pylons'
(p. 99), together with two related and almost equally famous
poems, 'The Landscape Near an Aerodrome' and 'The Express',
thinking about the implicit attitude of the poet towards the
objects he describes.

DISCUSSION

'The Pylons' deals with the impact of the new technology on
a landscape described in terms of smallness, privacy and inter-
relatedness: the cottages and the 'sudden hidden villages', may be
man-made, but they are compact, enclosed, and created out of the
very substance of the protective hills. The pylons, by contrast, are
alien features, structures of concrete and wire which, unlike the
hills, 'have no secret'. How do you respond to the poet's comparison

of these concrete pillars to 'nude, giant girls'? Strongly sexual, the image is perhaps less alluring than threatening; the 'small hills' appear deeply vulnerable in the face of this stern gigantism and, notwithstanding the explicit femininity of the forms, we may find ourselves envisaging their 'trek' as an assault akin to rape.

The third stanza confirms the threat to the intimate perspectives of the traditional rural landscape. The chestnut's 'customary root' initially suggests stability and sustenance derived from contact with the land and with the past; but the tree, like the valley in which it presumably stands, is 'mocked dry', its greenness vulnerable to the incursion of new forces.

As Spender goes on to define those forces, you may find your responses becoming less clear-cut. That the pylons are seen as in some sense antagonistic to life is plain enough; but they also manifest 'the quick perspective of the future'. 'Quick' means both 'fast' and 'living', and the insistence on vitality qualifies – though it doesn't of course negate – the suggestions of destruction which emerge so strongly from the third stanza. These new channels of energy actively supersede the old, gesturing prophetically towards a future which is evidently not unwelcome to the poet: although the verb 'dwarfs' reinforces some of the earlier suggestions of oppression, the lyrical flourish of the poem's conclusion provides a final sense of uplift.

I wonder if you feel, though, that there's something slightly suspect about this conclusion. I don't mean simply that you may not subscribe to the implied view that modern technology will lead us into a visionary world of heroic proportions but, more significantly, that the poet has achieved his superficially impressive effect by a kind of sleight of hand. What interests me about this poem is Spender's apparent reluctance to accept the pylons on their own terms: he assimilates them by defining them in terms of the organic, the natural. As feminine forms ('like nude, giant girls') they may be disturbing, but the simile undoubtedly softens their harsh outlines; while the high-rise cities of the future are veiled by clouds whose improbable, singular 'neck' provides an opportunity to evoke one of the most graceful of birds. The concluding image draws its power not from the pylons or the cities they anticipate, but from its reference to the natural world.

You might like to bear this point in mind as we go on to examine 'The Express' (p. 79), arguably the finest of the machine-poems of the 1930s. It's an impressively structured poem: you'll have seen how adroitly Spender builds up the impression of increasing speed, while at the same time developing the notion of the express train as a sentient embodiment of mystery and power.

I wonder if you're intrigued, as I am, by the sound of the poem. Try reading aloud the first three lines, with their emphatic plosives ('powerful', 'plain', 'pistons') coupled with the recurrent 'st' of 'first', 'manifesto', 'statement', 'pistons' and 'station'. The effect is to suggest the sound of a steam-engine as it begins to move, just as the later phrase 'retreats the elate metre' echoes, with equal appropriateness, the clatter of wheels on rails. To argue that these clusters are not accidental is not, of course, to suggest that the poet, in the act of writing, has consciously chosen each word for the sake of its sound (the creative process is usually far subtler than that) but I think you'll agree that the fruitful interrelationship of sound and imagery is not merely fortuitous.

The opening stage of the express train's journey is represented as a regal procession; Spender's later revelation that 'queen' in the third line carries some of its homosexual connotations[2] needn't radically affect our vision of the stately progress he describes. You may be struck by the phrase 'without bowing' which, in making the ostensibly unnecessary observation that the machine doesn't acknowledge its surroundings, actually reinforces the idea of non-mechanical response by suggesting that it might do so. And you'll notice that it's not only the express which possesses human attributes, but the surroundings too: the houses, like people gathered for a glimpse of royalty, 'humbly crowd' its route.

As the express gathers speed and moves beyond the confines of the cluttered town into 'open' landscapes, the description of its progress takes on quasi-mystical overtones, and the train's initial solidity gives way to something more ethereal. Spender's early poetry was often characterized by a Shelleyan yearning towards visionary manifestations of light, and you'll doubtless recognize the tendency here, in the train's 'luminous self-possession' as it 'plunges new eras of white happiness' or the 'streamline brightness' of its exhalations as it moves onward 'like a comet through flame'. I wonder if you know J. M. W. Turner's famous painting 'Rain, Steam and Speed – the Great Western Railway' which, although depicting a locomotive of a far earlier date, nevertheless offers interesting parallels with Spender's vision: it's a painting which shows a train hurtling, beneath the white haze of its own steam, down the luminous track of a railway bridge across the Thames; and I get from it the same sense of exhilaration at the partial dissolution of solid forms into a blur of speed and light.

How do you respond to the poem? Does the transfigured express seem to suggest a legitimate intensification of vision, or a failure to confront the true nature of the machine? You might find relevant the relationship between the conclusion of this poem and that of 'The Pylons': Spender's explicit assertion in 'The Express' is that the manifestations of the natural world cannot match those of the mechanical; but once again it's the poet's evocation of the natural – bird song, the 'bough/Breaking with honey buds' – which is responsible for the lyrical charge of the poem's closing lines.

'The Landscape Near an Aerodrome' (p. 82) opens with a similar assertion of the superiority of the mechanical to the natural: the aeroplane is not only 'more beautiful' than the moth which it partially resembles but also, less plausibly, softer. Spender is not, however, primarily concerned here with the machine itself, but with the landscape as seen from the elevated vantage-point which it offers its passengers.

Distance above the earth lends a kind of enchantment: the travellers are 'lulled by descent', while the land over which they have flown is described in terms of a gently receptive sensuality. As the distance diminishes, however, the travellers' eyes adjust to the mundane: the sight of the 'fraying edge' of the industrial townscape precipitates a shift of mood and imagery, and the relaxed tone and the images of easy movement give way to the disturbing suggestions of the 'chimneys like lank black fingers/Or figures frightening and mad' and the buildings 'like women's faces/ Shattered with grief'.

The enchantment is not quite over, but the phrase 'the last sweep of love' heralds its end: this is a consummation which brings the travellers down from their literally elevated state to the constraints of a harsh and disquieting world. The boys' cries, significantly likened to birds, are lost beneath the 'loud city', while the church obscures the already declining light. What do you take to be the significance of Spender's assertion that religion, as emblematized by the church, is 'larger' than the dark structures of the industrial landscape? You may be slightly disorientated at first by Spender's blurring of the distinction between the building itself and the abstraction it represents; but I think you'll recognize at once the implied suggestion that religion is a social force even more oppressively powerful than unenlightened industrialism.

Whether or not you believe that Spender's implicit criticism of religion is justified, you might like to consider whether it's well-made. My own feeling is that it seems to have been tacked on to the poem rather than to have emerged from it; is this your impression? Spender devoted much time during the 1930s to the attempt to square an active social conscience with an idealist view of the good poem as an entity 'complete in itself' and unconcerned with directing the course of everyday life: 'this is what people mean', he claimed, 'when they say that it is impossible to write propagandist poetry'.[3] Does his reference to religion at the end of this particular poem seem to you to be entirely non-directive? Does the poem fail in this respect to meet the poet's own criteria? More importantly, since you may not accept his rather extreme suggestion that 'separate poems are separate and complete and ideal worlds', do you yourself feel, as I do, that Spender's thinly veiled attack on religion creates a slight imbalance within the poem? Not because socio-religious comment has no place in poetry, but because, in this instance, that comment is not securely grounded in the poem as a whole.

Spender's social conscience took him briefly into the Communist Party and, perhaps more significantly in terms of his personal and artistic development, out to Spain, where the Civil War inspired some of his most deeply compassionate poetry. Although in Spain as an observer rather than as a combatant, he was acutely sensitive to the experience of those actively engaged in the fighting: poems such as 'Two Armies' and 'Ultima Ratio Regum' suggest nothing of that clinical detachment so characteristic of Auden's 'Spain'.

Let's look now at 'Two Armies' (p. 144), a poem which has strong affinities with some of the best poetry of the First World War, and particularly with the work of Wilfred Owen, a poet widely admired by Spender's generation. In his survey, *A Hope For Poetry*, Day Lewis claimed him, alongside Gerard Manley Hopkins and T. S. Eliot, as an immediate poetic ancestor,[4] while Auden quoted him in his 1933 poem 'Here on the cropped grass of the narrow ridge I stand'; and Spender himself has subsequently acknowledged that he and others were, during the 1930s, writing poetry 'profoundly influenced by the diction and attitudes of Wilfred Owen'.[5] If you know Owen's 'Anthem for Doomed Youth', you'll notice one particularly striking indication of that influence. Owen's 'What passing-bells for these who die as cattle?/Only the monstrous anger of the guns . . .' is almost certainly the source of these lines in 'Two Armies':

> . . . who can connect
> The inexhaustible anger of the guns
> With the dumb patience of these tormented animals?

DISCUSSION

'Two Armies' is a poem which clearly supports Spender's later claim that there was, to a generation influenced by Owen, 'something repugnant about the whole enterprise of writing poetry supporting our side against the other side'.[6] The title immediately suggests the accommodating nature of the poet's vision; and it's not simply a question of a vision which encompasses both factions, but of one which doesn't discriminate between them. Look at the beginning of the second stanza, with its emphatic 'All' followed by the assertion that 'each man hates the cause and distant words/ Which brought him here': the conflicting ideologies which have given rise to the war become worse than irrelevant to their representatives, who are in some sense drawn together by their common hatred of a singular, and therefore undifferentiated, 'cause'. Even specific incidents are confusingly unlocated: is the boy who hums the marching song to be identified with the novice who salutes, or is the poet describing two separate, if similar, incidents? On which side does the inappropriate display of enthusiasm occur? The uncertainty confirms the unimportance of faction in this arena of suffering humanity; and Spender underscores the point by describing the wounding of the over-zealous young soldier 'by those of his own side', an act which blurs, in a particularly disturbing way, the distinction between friend and foe.

But the blurring of distinction also has a more positive aspect. The penultimate stanza begins by suggesting the insignificance of the physical space separating the two armies: they are divided by 'a little walk'. Spender's choice of phrase is well judged: 'walk' suggests not only the space itself but the possibility of crossing it and, moreover, of doing so in an essentially casual and unthreatening manner. And that hint of *rapprochement* is followed by an explicit reference to the men's 'common suffering' which 'Whitens the air with breath and makes both one/As though these enemies slept in each others arms'. The men are united by shared experience, and the poet's vision of mingled breath, of bodies brought together in a quasi-sexual embrace, seems to hold out the hope of wholeness achieved through the effacement of divisive boundaries.

It's not, however, on this note of hope that Spender chooses to end the poem. The final stanza reasserts the dominance of death and destruction, by taking up and subverting the idea of friendship which has just been brought into play; the moon is, of course, 'friend' to raiding aircraft because she illuminates their targets. There's something deeply disquieting about the suggestion that even nature has been conscripted: a 'pilot' may simply be someone who guides others to their destination, but the context allows us to identify the moon even more closely with the airmen and with the devastation they create; and it is the brilliant but sinister play of moonlight which transforms the plain into a 'shining bone', emblematic of the death explicitly mentioned in the poem's concluding sentence.

'Two Armies' is a poem which derives much of its power from the breadth of its compassion, from its non-discriminatory pity for all those involved in the fighting. 'Ultima Ratio Regum' (p. 148) is apparently more specific in its focus, but you'll quickly realize that the young subject of Spender's moving elegy is a representative figure rather than a known and sharply defined individual. Again the poet reduces to irrelevance the question of political allegiance; the dead soldier might belong to either side, and our sympathies are enlisted on firmly non-partisan grounds.

We need to think for a moment about the poem's title. The proverbial Latin phrase means 'the last argument of kings' and refers to the use of armed force. The first line draws on the traditional connection but also suggests by its twisting of the phrase in translation (*'money's* ultimate reason') that the world of modern warfare is ruled by economic forces.

The first two stanzas emphasize the inappropriateness of the boy's death: he was, Spender insists, 'a better target for a kiss' than for a bullet, and his simple life was marginal to the pre-occupations of a threateningly sophisticated world. Look at the way in which, towards the end of the second stanza, our thoughts are turned back to the 'money' of the poem's first line: the 'gold' and the 'Stock Exchange rumour' function figuratively here, but are clearly crucial to a poem predicated on the idea of money's destructive power.

The third stanza cleverly sets images of the natural world to which the boy seems to belong alongside those of the brutal environment which has destroyed him. You may feel, as I do, that the scattering of petals by the breeze is subtly linked to the idea of monetary expenditure: the action is nature's innocuous parallel to the vicious commerce of war. And there are further parallels: the wall is 'unflowering' (although the primary suggestion of the word is of the absence of flowers, you might like to consider, in the context of the brutal violation depicted here, a possible association with 'deflowering') yet 'sprouts' with guns, whose bullets ironically recall the boy's rural background by 'scything' the grasses. The stanza's closing lines imply firstly a certain closeness between man and nature (the near-equation of flags and leaves, hands and branches) and ultimately, through the poignant obliquity of the rotting cap, nature's reassimilation of the human.

The final stanza reveals with particular clarity the poem's delicate balancing of passion and detachment. You'll remember Auden's injunction to 'Consider this ... As the hawk sees it or the helmeted airman'; and Spender's own request that we 'consider' may at first sight suggest something of the distance and coolness of Auden's perspective. You may be a little surprised to find him questioning not the moral acceptability of the killing but its economic justification; but you'll quickly appreciate the way in which the poet's 'reason', countering that of money in money's own terms, modulates into the open-mouthed cry of grief, despair and, arguably, moral outrage which concludes the poem.

Since Spender was not in Spain as a combatant, it was almost inevitable that he should feel himself to be in some sense marginal to events: asked at one point to fire a few shots into the enemy lines, he was suddenly aware of his status as 'visitor' to the trench in which he stood, and of the 'terrible frivolity' of his own brief and unwilling participation in the hostilities.[7] 'Port Bou' (p. 146), the third of the Spanish Civil War-inspired poems I'd like us to look at, seems to me to be largely concerned with that marginality, with the incompleteness of the poet's own engagement; perhaps you'd like to read the poem through carefully with this suggestion in mind.

DISCUSSION

You'll no doubt be familiar with the idea that the terms in which a description is couched may tell us as much about the writer himself as about his subject. What do you make of Spender's choice of images as he describes his surroundings in the first eight lines of this poem? Do those images seem to you to say anything about the poet's perception of his own relationship to the world? The description of the harbour waters emphasizes at once their near-identity with, and their partial separation from, the sea beyond; the illustrative description of the held pet evokes 'outer freedom' yet subtly insists on the animal's captivity. The waters may 'vibrate' to the open sea, yet there remains a sense that they are not quite one with that luminous expanse where 'ships and dolphins swim and above is the sun'. How far can these images be taken to represent the incomplete involvement of the poet himself?

Certainly Spender hints strongly at a resemblance between himself and the scene he describes: just as 'the earth-and-rock flesh arms of this harbour/Embrace but do not enclose' the harbour waters, so his own 'circling arms' lie on a newspaper characterized as 'empty' to a mind absorbed in the act of poetic creation. The parallel, reinforced towards the end of the poem by the pointed repetition of the phrase 'my circling arms', is obviously not accidental; and as he goes on to define more clearly his own marginal relationship to the war, we become more fully aware of the significance of his opening references to an outward urge circumscribed by pressures which preclude full engagement. The militiamen who briefly stop beside him refuse his proffered gift of the newspaper before driving on 'over the vigorous hill', leaving him behind; even the old, even women and children, are drawn out of the village to watch the firing practice on the headland, while the poet remains. The phrase 'at the exact centre' seems, in context, deeply ironic. This abandoned figure, companioned only by the 'disgraceful' dogs, is central to the village only in the most literal, geographical sense; it is his distance from the action, such as it is, which marks him out.

The action is not, of course, war itself, but firing practice; yet Spender's anxiety is real enough, and not entirely without justification. Not in immediate danger from the guns, he's nevertheless aware of the significance of their activity; and in defining, in the poem's concluding lines, the spasms of fear which pass through his body, he represents himself as passive victim of the weapons' intimidating power. Like the earlier reference to himself as a target, this description of a body penetrated – albeit not literally – by gunfire can be interpreted as an attempt to share the experience of those actively engaged in the war; but it's an attempt which, by implication, seems rather to emphasize the poet's distance from full involvement in the conflict.

Let's now consider 'An Elementary School Class Room in a Slum' (p. 51). At first sight a very different kind of poem, does it nevertheless have affinities with 'Port Bou'? Please read it now.

DISCUSSION

The children who sit at their lessons are circumscribed by the walls of their classroom and, beyond those walls, by the dismal townscape to which their poverty has consigned them. Again Spender opens the poem with an image of the sea: these children live 'far from gusty waves', from the free play of air and water. What is the effect of this brief reference to a world to which they have no access? The poet half-offers, half-denies the open prospect, presenting it in such a way as to emphasize its unavailability, and moving rapidly on to harsher realities; and this has its appropriateness for a poem centrally concerned with the idea of a freedom which is at once proffered and withheld.

In what terms are the children described? The dominant suggestion is of their sickliness, their failure to thrive. The pale faces are surrounded by hair 'like rootless weeds', the notion of rootlessness seeming to spread beyond its immediate context to define not the hair alone, but the children themselves, some of whom the poet goes on to describe individually. The tall girl's physique hints at an oppression she can barely sustain; the boy with 'rat's eyes' (rats are of course associated with cramped and unwholesome surroundings) is described as 'paper-seeming', the phrase picking up on the earlier suggestion of paleness as well as implying an unhealthy lack of solidity; and the crippled child manifests a hereditary sickness which we should certainly interpret literally, but which might suggest to you a social, as well as a parental, bequest.

The first stanza ends with a reference to the imaginary world of a child whose vision seems to carry him beyond the confines of the classroom; but the 'tree room' which his imagination occupies is explicitly defined as 'a dream', and we are recalled almost immediately to the 'sour cream walls' which actually surround him and his companions. Were you puzzled at first by the references to Shakespeare's head and the incongruous Tyrolese valley? By the time you reached the phrase 'open-handed map' you had probably realized that the poet was speaking of the pictorial decorations and teaching aids affixed to the classroom walls. Like the opening reference to the sea, these gesture outward to a world of wider possibilities: adjectives such as 'cloudless', 'civilized', 'flowery' and 'open-handed', very different from those which dominate the first stanza, suggest vistas at once attractive and expansive.

'And yet', Spender continues, 'for these/Children, these windows, not this world, are world.' The statement may initially seem a little confusing, but if you read carefully you'll see that 'these windows' are the actual windows of the room rather than the potentially liberating images on the walls while, conversely, 'this world' refers not to the children's immediate surroundings but to the expanded perspectives theoretically afforded by the revelatory map: the prospect for these children remains gloomily circumscribed, any suggestion of enlargement being, the poet argues, cruelly inappropriate to their circumstances.

The final stanza, however, returns to the possibility of escape from the 'foggy slum'. Spender's public voice seems perhaps rather strained as he addresses, with a touch of soap-box oratory, those representatives of the system ('governor, teacher, inspector, visitor') who might assist that escape; but his natural lyricism reasserts itself as he imagines an outward movement which breaches the confining structures of classroom, town and, by implication, society, carrying the children into an edenic world of freedom and light.

Let's turn now to 'Easter Monday' (p. 89), in which the city is initially characterized as corrosive, as a dusty arena in which the delicate vitality of fresh spring growth is quickly suppressed. The environment is a 'desert' not merely because those who normally work there have abandoned it (Easter Monday is, of course, a bank holiday) but also because of an inherent sterility; I think you'll agree that the notion of the city as a life-inhibiting wasteland operates strongly and reasonably straightforwardly in the poem's opening lines.

DISCUSSION

The picture is more complicated, however. How do you understand the architectural imagery here? If you find it a little confusing, this may be because Spender is mingling reference to the neo-classical architecture of the present-day city with an evocation of Grecian ruin, creating the impression that the city itself has collapsed. The acanthus leaf which 'shoots other crowns/Of grass and moss' is the carved decoration which surmounts the Corinthian columns; fallen, it lies among vegetation which may still be in some sense threatened by it (it's difficult to resist the negative suggestions of 'shoots') but which, unlike the leaves of the poem's opening lines, can perhaps now flourish. You'll notice the reference to sand, and to the 'empty endless suns'; but it might be argued that this desert, precisely because of the destruction of its buildings, holds promise of renewed life.

The shift to the 'green meadows' can be interpreted simply as a movement out from the city to the countryside, where the holiday-makers are taking their ease; but you might like to consider the possibility that Spender is also suggesting the establishment of a new order in the aftermath of the city's imagined destruction. As you'll know, 'the city' is a term sometimes used quite specifically to indicate the role of London as a centre for the nation's financial and business concerns; and the destruction of buildings (you may remember that the Bank of England has an imposing neo-classical facade) can be read as a metaphor for the collapse of the capitalist system. This reading is reinforced by Spender's particularization of the tweed-clad gentlemen as 'bulls' – a term used to denote those who speculate optimistically on the Stock Exchange; the landscape now held in the lenses of their gold-rimmed spectacles implies a desirable widening of horizons, an altered vision.

If you tend to think in tactile terms, you may have sensed a delicate relationship between the 'velvet' mountains and the 'furred bloom' of the peach in the poem's concluding line. The peach is broadly significant of a densely packed sweetness; you'll appreciate the further significance of its appropriation by the 'holiday hands' which, functioning 'like one hand', potently suggest the drawing

together of human activity in a single concerted and productive
enterprise.

In considering how much political weight you give to 'Easter
Monday', you may find it helpful to track down Spender's 'Oh
young men oh young comrades', with its deprecatory reference to
'financiers like fossils of bones in coal' and its depiction of those
who step forth from a sterile environment to 'sleep with friend on
hill'; or 'After they have tired of the brilliance of cities', in which
Spender imagines reaching a country far from that represented by
'works, money, interest, building' and 'the failure of banks', a
country in which 'light equal, like the shine from snow, strikes all
faces'. These are poems unmistakably marked by Spender's political
concerns; and I think you'll have little difficulty in recognizing the
relationship between them and 'Easter Monday'.

There are also certain resemblances between 'Easter Monday'
and the poem which follows it in the anthology, 'New Year'
(p. 90). Again the depiction of a sterile existence in urban surroundings is succeeded by a vision of regeneration in an essentially
rural environment, and again the suggestions are broadly political.

DISCUSSION

How do you understand the imagery of the poem's first line? The
year is 'turning' in the sense that the old year is giving place to the
new, and we might have in mind the image of a page being
turned; but to be 'at the centre' of its movement seems to suggest
rotation, so that we might also imagine the poet caught in the
whirlwind of history; it's an image which is perhaps reinforced by
the later reference to men being 'whirled' up to shallow sexual
liaisons in the town's high-rise buildings.

The poet's response to the polar bleakness of his world is not
to seek warmth, a quality represented in the second stanza by the
image of a man who 'burns endlessly/In the brandy pudding
crowned with holly'; the notion of seasonal festivity is dramatically
qualified by the suggestion of eternal torment, and it is Spender's
resolve to turn away from those apparent consolations which are,
in fact, a kind of hell, embracing instead the rigours not only of
the present winter but also the chiding snowfalls of 'future
disappointment'.

Spender was much concerned at this stage of his development
with the confrontation of a potentially destructive reality. His
critical study of modern literature, published in 1935, bore the
title *The Destructive Element*, the phrase itself being drawn from
Joseph Conrad's injunction: 'In the destructive element immerse'.

It's just such an immersion which is envisaged in 'New Year', as
the poet requests that he should be cloaked in – that is, enfolded
by – the various forms of failure and disorder which characterize
contemporary society. If this request seems at first sight difficult to
understand, you may find it helpful to reflect on a passage from
The Destructive Element in which Spender links Auden's *The
Orators* with Rainer Maria Rilke's *Notebook of Malte Laurids
Brigge*, arguing that both writers advance the view that

> illness of the body ... is to be regarded with relief as a recognizable
> symptom, or even in some cases with gratitude as an effective cure.[8]

If we translate this interpretation of bodily illness into broader
terms, we'll perhaps understand more clearly the poet's desire to
be enveloped by the manifestations of a sick society. As Spender
himself suggests in the introduction to his study, immersion in the
destructive element may be the necessary prelude to 'emerging at
the other side'.[9]

Although there's a certain inwardness implicit in the poet's
location of the new world within the heart, you'll appreciate that
the idea of emergence is strongly present in the concluding stanza
of the poem. As in 'Easter Monday', activity is both fruitful and
concerted: the singular 'Will' and 'hand' emphasize the common
concern of those who answer 'the harvests of obliteration' with
action which, if rather vaguely defined, suggests a more productive
husbandry. You'll notice too the suggestion of geographical enlargement as the image of the inhibiting town gives place to that of a
dynamic force ploughing 'across the nations'.

The urge towards enlargement which we've already seen
exemplified in 'An Elementary School Class Room in a Slum' and
'Easter Monday' is fundamental to Spender's poetic vision: 'There
is never a wide enough space', he wrote in 'Variations on my Life',
'never a white enough light'. 'I Think Continually' (p. 111) is a
poem much concerned with extremes of space and light, a hymn
to the 'truly great' who 'in their lives fought for life'. Their actions
and achievements are seen as a reflection of their souls' previous
experience of a world where both light and time are 'endless';
their lips, 'still touched with fire', convey truths from beyond the
temporal world.

Who are the 'truly great'? Spender is unspecific, and those
coming across the poem on its first appearance in book form,
in *New Signatures*, might well have interpreted it in the light
of Michael Roberts' assessment of another of Spender's poems
published in that volume, as an example of 'poetry ... turned to
propaganda'.[10] Spender is likely to have been thinking primarily

of great poets and musicians: the references to song in the first
stanza are suggestive, and one might reasonably posit a connection
with 'Beethoven's Death Mask' which appeared with 'I Think
Continually' in Spender's first collection, and which ends with an
impressionistic depiction of music as a sun whose intensity obliterates earthly lights; or with 'Hoelderlin's Old Age', in which the
mad poet's soul 'sings/Burning vividly in the centre of a cold sky'.
But Spender's contemporaries would not, I think, have been wrong
to relate 'I Think Continually' to the poet's political concerns; like
so many of the poems of the period it at once touched, and was
touched by, the broadly liberative impulses of a socially conscious
generation.

It may be helpful to bear Spender's poetry in mind if you're
ever tempted towards simplistic assessments of the generation's
political allegiances. Like much of the best writing of the decade,
it is deeply informed by moral and aesthetic concerns which
undoubtedly found a political focus but which actually transcended
contemporary politics. The point is an important one, for it implies
a poetry less rigidly confined by its period, more broadly relevant
to the human condition, than we are sometimes led to believe.

4. A Sense of Loss: Louis MacNeice

Writing in 1938 in *Modern Poetry*, a survey of the work of his
contemporaries, Louis MacNeice noted a variety of influences on
his own work, including the fact that he had been brought up in
Northern Ireland; that his father was a clergyman; that his mother
had died when he was small; that part of his childhood had been
marked by repression; and that his marriage had recently ended in
divorce. All poetry is of course informed by the life of its author,
but there's a particularly strongly autobiographical cast to

MacNeice's writing; your understanding of the poems would be enhanced by a reading of his unfinished biography, *The Strings are False*, arguably the best of the memoirs produced by this literary generation.

You might also like to look at MacNeice's 'Carrickfergus', a poem not included in Skelton's anthology, but to be found in both MacNeice's *Collected* and *Selected Poems*. From its direct opening ('I was born in Belfast . . .') to its final stanza ('I went to school in Dorset . . .'), this is an overtly autobiographical piece; and though we shan't be examining it in detail here, it might be helpful to note the poem's emphasis on separation. MacNeice's Anglican background is not a source of sustenance, but the reason he feels himself 'Banned for ever from the candles of the Irish poor'; and the ambivalent conclusion comprehends a powerful awareness of severance from a world which perhaps, to appropriate a phrase from one of MacNeice's later poems, 'was never home' ('Nostalgia'). 'There was always a sense of loss',[1] he wrote of his early childhood; and the sense of loss, actual or threatened, underlies a remarkably large proportion of his poetry.

We can begin with 'Christina' (p. 256), a poem whose first three stanzas directly recall one of the poet's childhood experiences; the relevant sentence in the autobiography is an ostensibly dispassionate account of an apparently minor event:

> Later I took my sister's doll, with a pink frilled dress and big blue eyes, and built her a house out of coloured bricks on the table but she was too heavy for the house, the walls fell down and over the edge of the table and she went with them and broke and was hollow inside.[2]

What does MacNeice do with this experience in 'Christina'? This is clearly far more than a recollection of childhood loss; it's a poem about the continuing relevance of such loss in the adult world.

DISCUSSION

What are the implications of the poem's opening phrase? If someone tells us that everything began well, there is usually a strong suggestion of subsequent deterioration; the first stanza's depiction of a child whose playful acts of destruction can always be remedied is shadowed from the outset by the hint that things have now changed, that he can no longer simply pick up the pieces and start again. The point is reinforced by the description of the breaking of the doll: split open to reveal her own hollowness, she

implicitly repudiates the idea that the child might go on dressing
and undressing her for ever, to the accompaniment of her fixed
smile.

In his autobiography MacNeice tells us simply that the doll
wore a pink frilled dress, while the poem focuses closely on her
underwear and on the child's intimate play with her. I think you'll
be aware, even on a first reading, of the sexual overtones of the
dressing and undressing; and the final stanza picks up those
suggestive threads as it describes a sexual encounter in the adult
world, an encounter which, we are explicitly told, reactivates the
childhood memory. The early intimations of loss at once illuminate
and are illuminated by the adult's experience of despoliation and
disillusion.

Loss is the theme, too, of 'The Sunlight on the Garden'
(p. 273), a tautly written lament for a vanishing way of life. It was
MacNeice's gift to be able to draw together the public and the
personal in a way unmatched by most of his contemporaries; and
while the 'you' of the final stanza suggests a concluded personal
relationship, the reference to the message of 'every evil iron/Siren'
makes it clear that the poem's elegiac mood has as much to do
with the threat of war as with lost love. Please read the poem
now, spending some time over the form of the stanzas, which is
more complex than you may have realized on first reading.

DISCUSSION

In addition to following, with the final words of each line, a pattern
which we can conventionally represent as *abcbba*, MacNeice
rhymes or half-rhymes the first word of the second line with the
last word of the first, and the first word of the fourth with the last
word of the third. You'll notice too that he works to a clear-cut
metrical scheme, even the superbly judged variation of each stanza's
penultimate line establishing its own pattern within the poem as a
whole. A classicist by training, MacNeice had a fine ear for, and a
deep interest in, the music of verse, devoting a chapter of *Modern
Poetry* to the subject of rhythm and rhyme and stating his own
preference 'for poetry which is musical' but significantly adding
that 'the characteristics of this music are not superficial prettiness
or smoothness'.[3]

Would you agree with me that 'The Sunlight on the Garden'
is far from superficial? The grave formality of its music is actually
an integral and important aspect of the poem, and much of the
taut energy I find here seems to derive from MacNeice's bringing
of powerful emotions under the control implicit in a firmly defined

framework. Formally impeccable, readily accessible (with the possible exception of the phrase 'We are dying, Egypt, dying', a modified borrowing from Shakespeare's *Antony and Cleopatra*, the content is unlikely to have presented you with any problems of interpretation) this is a poem which might well satisfy the most hardened traditionalist; yet it is also very much of its time, neatly encapsulating one of the dominant moods of what C. Day Lewis referred to as 'a tricky, darkening decade'.

'The Sunlight on the Garden' was written in 1937, but MacNeice was in fact conscious of the threatening darkness from a far earlier stage in the decade. Let's turn now to 'An Eclogue for Christmas' (p. 207), written in 1933. The first speaker defines the present as 'an evil time', while the second envisages society going down 'like paleolithic man/Before some new Ice Age or Genghiz Khan'. In this, MacNeice is perhaps to some extent echoing his Virgilian models; but he is also clearly expressing a vision of his own social and historical context.

DISCUSSION

Like five of Virgil's ten *Eclogues*, 'An Eclogue for Christmas' is in the form of a dialogue. The two speakers, while sharing a vision of civilization's decline, have apparently sharply differentiated reactions to the world's degeneration, speaker A turning for solace to the jazzy, hectic life of the city, while speaker B seeks refuge in the countryside. Yet it is noteworthy that B addresses A as 'Analogue of me', suggesting a close correspondence between the two; one might indeed interpret the phrase as a hint that the speakers represent complementary facets of the poet's own mind.

What is abundantly clear is that neither the country nor the city offers any hope of salvation. Speaker B checks his interlocutor's impulse to turn to him, insisting that the rural world which he himself represents 'will not yield you any sanctuary' and suggesting that 'to die *in situ*' – that is, in the places they currently occupy – is the best to which they can aspire: 'One place is as bad as another', he remarks, neatly inverting a familiar cliché. The response of speaker A is to delineate the urban world in terms which clearly establish its inadequacy as refuge: the music and lights accentuate rather than conceal the superficial and fragmentary nature of contemporary society. However far the speaker may seem to have moved from the 'bombs and mud and gas' which arguably represent not only the memory of the past war but fear of a future one, he has evidently failed to provide himself with any substantial bulwark against the disturbing pressures of an age whose fragmentation is mirrored in the visual arts: the innocence and clarity of form of Picasso's early paintings has given way to cubism's 'broken facets'.

I wonder if the description of contemporary urban life struck you as ambivalent? Phrases like 'butter-smooth trulls' and 'a slick beauty of gewgaws' undoubtedly convey contempt, but also seem to me to suggest a certain relish. The word 'beauty' isn't completely compromised by the qualifying 'slick'; and when MacNeice refers to the city's beauty for the second time, there's no mistaking the delight implicit in the description which follows: the globed lamps on the traffic islands, the luminous haze which seems, in its purring and crooning, to express love, the light flashed from the passing buses, all appear here to represent something more than a merely superficial and deceptive allure. If we register the negative suggestion of the adjective 'narcotic' as applied to this urban beauty, we're nevertheless obliged to give due weight to 'noble' and 'tall' as well as to the unmistakably celebratory 'glory like chrysanthemums'. It's worth emphasizing that the conclusion of the poem, considerably more upbeat than its opening, suggests the desirability of celebration, whether of England's rural landscapes or of 'the cult of every technical excellence': the expressed hope that these 'so ephemeral things' might nevertheless be 'somehow permanent' is the indirect tribute of a poet whose pessimism is counterbalanced by the pleasure he derives from the phenomenal world.

You'll find a more detailed account of urban life in 'Birmingham' (p. 80). MacNeice spent six years as a lecturer at Birmingham University; he was later to claim that he and his wife 'ignored our Birmingham context as much as possible . . . and spent most of our free time driving into Shropshire',[4] but the poem itself suggests the writer's genuine, if implicitly critical, interest in his urban surroundings. Rural Shropshire may have had more obvious attractions, but the life of an industrial city seems, in its own way, to have proved inspiring. Please now read the poem.

DISCUSSION

MacNeice's acute eye for contemporary tackiness is immediately apparent here. It's not simply his sharp delineation of detail which is likely to impress you, however, but his suggestions of incongruity: the 'Cubical scent-bottles artificial legs arctic foxes and electric mops' are thrown together, significantly unpunctuated, like so much rubbish; again we sense the poet's relish, but the negative implications are unmistakable. Even more striking in this respect is the third stanza: read its single rambling sentence carefully, registering the way in which it reflects the incoherence which, initially attributed to the shopgirls' faces, seems to sprawl out through juxtaposition and comparison to encompass the 'gewgaws', the stained glass windows 'broken' by their own leading and, since the punctuation doesn't permit foreclosure, all the details bundled into the remainder of this syntactically loose and erratic stanza. You might have been tempted on a first reading to regard the stanza as an example of careless writing; but a little thought – as well as a wider reading of MacNeice's poetry – should convince you that the poet is actually creating a structural parallel to the cluttered vistas and jerry-built housing of the city and its suburbs.

Alongside the suggestions of tackiness, you'll have noted the references to nobler traditions and ideas: the policeman, for example, is likened to 'monolith Pharaoh', to the imposing figure of an Egyptian ruler; we might perhaps (especially if we read 'monolith' literally) see this figure as one of those striking hieratic statues whose solidity and durability would seem a direct reproach to the shallowly rooted society MacNeice depicts in this poem. Similarly, the reference to the Platonic Forms – that is, to the manifestations of an ideal or essential reality – plainly highlights perceived inadequacies: there's a mocking sarcasm in the poet's assertion that these elusive ideals are being pursued 'With wireless and cairn terriers and gadgets', as well as in his subsequent reference to the citizens' attempts 'to find God and score one over the neighbour/By climbing tentatively upward on jerry-built beauty and sweated labour'. Idealism may have its place; but not, MacNeice half-humorously suggests, in the suburbs of Birmingham.

Yet I wonder if you feel, as I do, that there's a subtle change of mood in the final stanza. It's as though, having aired his negative feelings about the city, MacNeice finds himself at last able to write more lyrically about his subject. The 'insipid colour' of the third stanza now gives way to the richness of a sky 'plum after sunset, merging to duck's egg, barred with mauve' and the vivid 'Creme-de-menthe or bull's blood' of the traffic lights. You might notice too that the characterization of the cars' headlights as 'pentecost-like' evokes the holy spirit with little if any of the sarcasm of the earlier reference to God. This isn't to say that MacNeice's vision of the city has changed entirely: the trams which move 'like vast sarcophagi' inevitably suggest the living death of those city-dwellers who ride in them, while the 'sullen' factory chimneys and 'sleep-stupid' faces of the workers bear witness to a world of dull routine. But I think you'll have little difficulty in interpreting this final stanza in a fairly positive light, as a guarded celebration of the variegated life of a large city.

'London Rain' (p. 278) is defined by its title as another city poem, and the first stanza presents us with an economically delineated London streetscape; but we quickly realize that the city is not the poem's primary focus, but functions as a backdrop to more personal concerns. Please now read the poem.

DISCUSSION

You'll have recognized in 'An Eclogue for Christmas' MacNeice's liking for debate; and his tendency to express his awareness of life's complexity through dialogue is apparent in other poems of the period (you'll find three more eclogues in the *Collected Poems*) as well as in *I Crossed the Minch*, a prose account of a journey to the Hebrides, in which MacNeice engages in an occasionally witty and sometimes petulant argument with his Guardian Angel. 'London Rain' isn't strictly a dialogue, but clearly represents an internal debate: in weighing up the respective claims of logic and lust, or of God and 'No-God', the poet draws attention not merely to the necessity of moral choice, but to the difficulty of choosing.

Part of the difficulty lies in the fact that logic and lust, far from making rival claims as one might suppose, work as a persuasive double-act: the disorderly passions, which MacNeice characterizes as 'The randy mares of fancy/The stallions of the soul' or as a rider of those animals, are actually 'reinforced by logic'. The argument advanced by logic is both seductive and superficially clever: if God exists, he will pardon our sins while, if he doesn't, we can behave as we like. Does this argument convince you? You might perhaps be tempted to ask whether God, supposing Him to exist, is necessarily infinitely forgiving; or you might want to argue that morality shouldn't be dependent on a system of rewards and punishments. MacNeice himself seems to come close to the latter position in his statement that 'We need no metaphysics/To sanction what we do', but goes even further. Abstract philosophical speculation, he suggests, is a less reliable guide than direct experience of a world which exists as a pre-ordained entity yet is in some sense responsive to our actions: 'The world is what was given/The world is what we make.' The poem's conclusion follows naturally from this perception: fancy and speculation give way in the final stanza to acknowledgement of the poet's immediate surroundings – 'the falling London rain' – and the quiet acceptance implied in sleep.

We can now consider 'Meeting Point' (p. 192), a love poem

whose relatively sophisticated structure, like that of 'The Sunlight on the Garden', contains but in no way compromises a potent emotional force. Containment is, indeed, the theme of the poem: the experience shared by the two lovers has been miraculously abstracted from the normal flow of things, existing in the parenthesis created by time's absence. The concept is recurrent in MacNeice's poetry, negatively viewed in 'Ode' (CP 54), where the poet asserts that 'bottled time turns sour upon the sill', but revealed as elusively desirable in 'Trilogy for X' (CP 88), in which, from the vulnerable enclave of the 'hour of quiet after passion', he imagines keeping 'this door for ever/Closed on the world, its own world closed within it'.

DISCUSSION

'Meeting Point' represents MacNeice's most sustained treatment of these ideas. The couple in the coffee shop exist in a state of highly charged suspension, 'neither up nor down', while objects around them are struck into stasis: 'Somebody stopped the moving stairs.' The image of the soundless bell, arrested in the act of chiming, is a particularly vivid representation of a state sometimes achieved by mystics and drug-takers as well as lovers, a state which may involve a sense not merely of time's suspension but of the erosion of spatial boundaries as the observer merges with the observed ('There were ... two people with one pulse') or as past or future events are drawn into the timeless present. Here the music of the stream, presumably a feature of an earlier walk, perpetuates itself incongruously among the furniture of the coffee shop, while the ash on the girl's cigarettes recedes – according to my reading – into its own origins. Tobacco doesn't of course grow on 'tropic trees', and my interpretation of the sixth stanza hinges on the supposition that MacNeice was either ignorant of this or was prepared to sacrifice botanical accuracy for the sake of his rhyme; if you find this supposition implausible you'll need to look for another way of interpreting the lines.

Have you noticed the way in which, by rounding off the action (or inaction) of each stanza with a line which directly repeats the opening, MacNeice offers a structural representation of those suggestions of parenthesized experience which constitute the theme of the poem? Whatever goes on within the frame provided by the opening and closing lines, the form of the poem conspires with its explicit meaning to insist that, after all, time can 'stop like this'. 'Meeting Point' seems to me to be a remarkable assertion of the possibility of the impossible, a momentarily confident statement that the hope so cautiously expressed in 'An Eclogue for Christmas' – that the ephemeral might be 'somehow permanent' – is in some profound sense realizable.

Most of MacNeice's explorations of the theme are, however, marked by a poignant sense of the vulnerability of the islands we create for ourselves. The reasons for this are doubtless to be found partly in MacNeice's personal history, but we can hardly ignore the socio-political pressures which clearly inform, for example, the conclusion of his verse letter to W. H. Auden, 'Postscript to Iceland':

> Our prerogatives as men
> Will be cancelled who knows when;
> Still I drink your health before
> The gun-butt raps upon the door.

The image of the gun recurs in 'Prognosis' (p. 277), as MacNeice attempts to read a future personified by an incursive stranger, a messenger who may come either with 'a promise in his palm' or 'a gun in his holster'. Written only a few months before the outbreak of war, this is a simple but disturbing representation of a world in which everything seems uncertain except the imminence of significant change.

The futility of people's efforts to insulate themselves from a threatening and unstable environment is the central concern of 'The British Museum Reading Room' (p. 124), also written in the immediate run-up to war. The description of the readers emphasizes at once that they are 'haunted'; how do you understand this? The matter becomes clearer as we move on to the concluding lines of the first stanza, with their suggestion that the reading room represents the hope of refuge from an unspecific, but by definition malevolent, 'demon'.

DISCUSSION

Does your reading of the final phrase of the first stanza add anything to the opening passage in which the readers, in their 'hive-like dome' are likened to bees? If honey represents the richness or sweetness of their reading, what is the significance of the accumulated wax? In view of MacNeice's explicit reference here to the readers' desire to 'deaden/The drumming of the demon in their ears', it seems reasonable to see this wax in part as a means of stopping the ears – as a more intimate counterpart to the books' insulation of the walls. You might go on to ask yourself whether the phrase implies that the demon is itself located in the ear, or merely that its drumming resonates there; the former interpretation would reinforce the poem's strong suggestion that the attempt to escape is ultimately doomed.

The library users are defined in the second stanza in terms which accentuate their distance from the modern world; they wear 'pince-nez, period hats or romantic beards', the trappings of a past age. Like bats enclosed in their own furled wings, some are 'Folded up in themselves in a world which is safe and silent'. Do you take the suggestion of security at face-value? Even at this stage in the poem it's difficult to do so; and the final stanza seems radically subversive of any such notion. As we shift our attention from the reading room to the flight of steps outside the museum, we are likely to be struck at first by a sense of light and vitality: courting pigeons figure elsewhere in MacNeice's poetry as emblems of untrammelled living. But alongside the pigeons' courtship we are forced to register the brooding presence of the museum's totem poles, explicitly associated with terror; and the 'guttural sorrow of the refugees'. How do you respond to the imagery of the two final lines? The 'foreign faces', described in terms which you may perhaps associate with the iconography of the totem poles, are clustered at the entrance to the supposed sanctuary, bringing with them a sense of disturbance, hints of a dark world of persecutions and pogroms. The introverted readers – also, in their own way, refugees – are, by implication, themselves under threat.

Autumn Journal, MacNeice's long, discursive sequence of 1938–39, is deeply coloured by the poet's awareness that external pressures are bringing to an end an easy and insular way of life. In section VIII he looks back on life with his former wife:

> We slept in linen, we cooked with wine
>   We paid in cash and took no notice
> Of how the train ran down the line
>   Into the sun against the signal.

Now, however, he can no longer find refuge: he has 'No wife, no ivory tower, no funkhole', and crisis, manifested in protest meetings, the voice of Hitler on the wireless and the felling of trees on Primrose Hill to make way for a gun emplacement, 'hangs/Over the roofs like a Persian army'. Please look now at *Autumn Journal* XV (p. 170).

DISCUSSION

The poem portrays a society dedicated to hectic and superficial forms of enjoyment as a means of avoiding – or at least concealing from itself – the manifestations of crisis. 'Shelley and jazz and lieder and love and hymn-tunes': the section's opening line suggests the shallow, undiscriminating frenzy with which the revellers approach their cultural entertainments. They reach out with similar lack of discrimination for alcohol, for the stimulus of an aphrodisiac and for the narcotic pleasures of 'lotus', the plant which, according to Homer, induces in those who eat it a sweet forgetfulness of all care and responsibility; the hackneyed bar-room phrase 'Give me the same again', juxtaposed with the reference to the lotus, reinforces the impression of a coarse and undiscerning quest for pleasure. And MacNeice goes on to create a haphazard collage of 'sensations': erotic poetry; a muse who, seductively decked out in the height of expensive thirties fashion, supersedes the straitlaced muse of the past; the delirium of speed on the motor-circuit; wild discourse across the telegraph wires; murder; 'Strip-tease, fireworks, all-in wrestling, gin'. Sex in this world of mere sensation is crude and vicious: the speaker rejects a houri – one of the pleasure-giving women of the Mohammedan paradise – on the grounds that she would be 'too easy', opting instead for the virginal nun, and going on to suggest a further act of desecration. A reredos is the ornamental screen behind the altar: the suggestion is that, in the quest for sensation, nothing is sacred.

But look how the tone of the poem changes after the reference to drinking at 'the Hangman's Gate'. By envisaging this act of defiance, clearly intended as a challenge to the powers of death, the speaker inadvertently lets in the spectres he has been at such pains to exclude. How do you interpret the sombre procession of hanged men? If your answer to that question is that you're uncertain of their precise significance, this seems an entirely appropriate response; MacNeice clearly intends the vision to remain suggestively unspecific. The setting may be in part mediaeval but it is, confusingly, illuminated by modern neon lights, and when the speaker himself probes the identity of the figures, the outlines of their features are uncertain; the childhood nightmare, Christ's betrayer and the modern soldier are all, it is implied, comprehended in the disquietingly familiar faces.

What follows is an increasingly frenetic attempt to block the incursive horrors: 'Take no notice of them', urges the speaker, turning again to the distractions of a thoughtlessly materialistic society. You'll notice the hysterical tone of his discourse as, following his own advice not to stop talking, he attempts to convince himself firstly that the figures will vanish if ignored and secondly, that they can't possibly exist in any case. The logic of his argument may strike you as shaky, and this is of course the point.

The popular form of Heraclitus' assertion that 'we could not step twice into the same rivers' jostles with a reformulation of one of the saying of Christ (the half-echo of 'Sufficient unto the day is the evil thereof' significantly perturbs the blander surface of 'Sufficient to the moment is the moment') but there is no refuge either in chopped logic or in nursery-rhyme prattle ('This little lady has a fetish . . .'): the section's last line informs us, with chilling simplicity, that the spectres are still there.

Concerned though it is with a nightmare world lurching helplessly towards war, *Autumn Journal* is by no means a uniformly bleak document. Time and again, MacNeice's affection for the ordinary activities of everyday life gives a sense of uplift to the sequence, as when, for example, he describes himself driving by night 'Among red and amber and green, spears and candles,/ Corkscrews and slivers of reflected light/In the mirror of the rainy asphalt' (*Autumn Journal* XIV) or 'sneezing in the morning sunlight or smelling the bonfire/Over a webbed lawn and the naked cabbage plot (*Autumn Journal* XVIII). Or there's the optimism which surfaces in *Autumn Journal* III (p. 45) as the poet argues his way through his own inertia and self-interest towards a more positive vision of the world.

Perhaps you'd like to read through *Autumn Journal* III now. When, in the next chapter, we move on to an examination of Day Lewis' visions of regeneration in *The Magnetic Mountain*, you might like to think back to this section of *Autumn Journal*. I think you'll be struck by the relative thoughtfulness of MacNeice's argument, as well as by the guarded modesty of his conclusion. Would you agree with me that such optimism as emerges here is achieved with evident difficulty, and is all the more convincing for that?

DISCUSSION

The section begins with a description of those whose summer holidays have recently given them a taste of freedom, but who now have to return to a dull routine; MacNeice's assertion that they have managed to smuggle in 'a little/*Joie de vivre*' playfully suggests the scarcity of joy in their everyday lives. There is, admittedly, some solace for these people at the end of the working day, but it is a solace defined as evasive: 'self-glory/Or self-indulgence, blinkers on the eyes of doubt.'

The image of the blinkers – literally the leather patches used to restrict a horse's vision – leads naturally into the reference to the majority's being 'born and bred to harness'. If you're troubled at this point by what you see as hints of a patrician scorn for the masses, you should bear in mind that MacNeice will, as his argument progresses, go on to suggest that his own vision and action are similarly impeded. Nor is he slow to acknowledge the role of those who work towards 'a better Kingdom', a kingdom which although at present inadequately represented ('sketched in air', perhaps suggesting the gesticulations of those engaged in political debate, clearly implies a certain insubstantiality, while the daubed slogans are explicitly defined as travesties) may ultimately be more firmly embodied in men's lives.

You'll notice in what cautious terms MacNeice couches his vision of social regeneration: his anticipation of a society in which 'skill will no longer languish nor energy be trammelled' defines itself largely through reference to actual oppression and inequality. And he goes on, in a manner which may remind you of the internalized debate in 'London Rain', to accuse himself, through the imaginary figure of 'the tempter', of precisely the kind of exploitative attitudes which help to perpetuate the system he deplores. As the argument unfolds, you'll perhaps get a sense of genuine struggle, of the poet's using his verse not as a vehicle for ideas more or less clearly formulated from the outset but, more dynamically, as a means of active exploration.

Why does he characterize his self-accusation as a form of temptation? The answer isn't immediately apparent, but becomes clearer as he proceeds. His own complicity with the corrupt system – his desire for irresponsible power in both personal and more broadly social relationships – is undeniable; but, he goes on to argue, this mustn't be regarded as an excuse for inaction: the temptation he has to overcome is to indulge in that 'worst of all/ Deceits' by which, pleading unworthiness for the task, men justify their reluctance to change either themselves or their environment.

To 'turn your face to the wall' means to give up, in the manner of a dying man. Here, however, the phrase 'lying easy' suggests a more culpable turning away, while the implicit suggestions of blocked vision recall the earlier image of blinkered eyes. MacNeice's plea, at the poem's conclusion, is for a counteractive broadening of vision ('may I . . . look up and outwards') and for corresponding action: 'may my feet follow my wider glance'. The tone is still cautious – look how he checks the momentum of that final sentence by introducing the parenthetical phrase 'with time and luck' – and progress is envisaged as difficult; but the section nevertheless ends on an affirmative note, with a strong suggestion of man's capacity for personal and social development.

Autumn Journal VI (p. 160) describes the visit MacNeice

made to Spain in the Easter of 1936; his companion was Anthony
Blunt, the art historian whose espionage on behalf of Russia was
to create such a stir when it was revealed in 1979. The description
is retrospective, an irritable travelogue which takes on deeper
resonances as MacNeice reinterprets his experience from a position
of greater awareness.

DISCUSSION

It's not that the signs of disorder weren't visible at the time of
MacNeice's visit; they were there in abundance, and when he
refers to the 'writings on the walls' he is not simply drawing
attention to the presence of political graffiti but playing on the
proverbial phrase 'the writing is on the wall' – meaning that the
approach of disaster is both evident and irresistible. Nevertheless,
it was the rain which seemed at the time to pose the greatest
problem 'for a tripper'. MacNeice pointedly insists on this term,
with all its suggestions of limited engagement and superficial
understanding, observing that 'All that the tripper wants is the
status quo/Cut and dried for trippers'. There's no mistaking the
self-criticism here: you'll perhaps have picked up on the poet's use
of the adverb 'glibly' in describing his discussion of Spanish
business sense, and you'll readily appreciate the implied inadequacy
of the response which defines the newspapers, with their disturbing
freight of 'party politics and blank invective' as 'a lark'.

The emphasis on the superficial is recurrent: Spain's representation of its own former glory is defined as a 'veneer', a skin
incapable of holding together the 'rotten guts and crumbled bones'
of a degenerate body, while MacNeice's retrospective analysis
defines the nation's scenery as a 'painted hoarding'. With the
benefit of hindsight, the poet is able to locate the previously
unrecognized activity of 'the peoples' mind . . . tunnelling like a
mole to day and danger'; but the significance of the mob outside a
ransacked church or of the drunkard's 'blood-lust' seems to have
eluded him at the time. 'Not realizing', 'not knowing', the tourists
have departed casually from a country whose problems were 'not
our business'; the section's energies derive largely from the tension
between that view and the poet's subsequent understanding of
Spain's relevance to the world at large.

In a prefatory note to *Autumn Journal*, MacNeice argued
that the journal was a form in which 'a man writes what he feels
at the moment; to attempt scientific truthfulness would be –
paradoxically – dishonest'. The picture is perhaps complicated a
little by those passages which are, like section VI, present reflec-

tions on past events; and you might also want to argue that what we feel is inevitably changed by the act of writing it down. Nevertheless, I think you'll agree that the sequence gives a very strong impression of truthfulness to the moment. I spoke just now of the way in which the verse seems to embody the very process of exploration; and you might like to reflect on other aspects of its arresting immediacy.

Have you thought at all about the sequence's tone? Easy, conversational, it surely contributes substantially to the effect of immediacy. Were you aware, in your reading, of the deftness with which MacNeice at once establishes and subtly subverts his peculiarly hypnotic rhythms? It's a kind of writing which perhaps looks easier than it is: fluent, apparently relaxed, yet proving on examination to be the work of a skilled craftsman with a highly developed structural sense.

You may have made similar observations about 'An Eclogue for Christmas' and 'Birmingham'; and you might like to turn now, with the question of tone still in mind, to 'Bagpipe Music' (p. 72). Part nonsense, part high-spirited social comment, the poem seems to have about it a certain throwaway carelessness. But look more closely: a mere scattering of the apparently slapdash rhymes ('rickshaw/peepshow', 'python/bison', 'sofa/poker') might suggest insouciance on the part of the poet; but when we find every rhyme in the poem jarring in similar fashion, we're bound to consider the likelihood that he has actually worked with some care to achieve his effect. The carelessness, I would suggest, is only apparent, a means of conveying the slapdash attitudes of a public eager, like the speaker in *Autumn Journal* XV, for cheap sensation in a materialist world.

One of the advantages of reading a reasonably wide selection of verse by a particular poet – or, indeed, by a number of poets whose work is in some sense related – is that our understanding of each individual poem is enhanced by the knowledge we've accumulated. By referring back to the poems we've already discussed, you'll be able to see more clearly the significance of the hectic high-jinks of 'Bagpipe Music', to appreciate more fully the darkness beneath the glitter. The image of the falling glass – that is, barometer – in the final stanza is, I think, the key to a poem which, like so much written by MacNeice and his contemporaries during the 1930s, is fundamentally reflective of a generation's sense of actual loss and imminent disaster.

5. Between Two Fires: C. Day Lewis

Looking back on the 1930s in his 1960 autobiography, *The Buried Day*, C. Day Lewis claimed that he had written 'only two political poems of any value';[1] since most of the poems he wrote during the decade were either directly or obliquely politicial, this is a statement of some significance.

The two poems to which he refers are 'The Conflict' and 'In Me Two Worlds', both accurately described by Day Lewis himself as 'poems of the divided mind'. Although 'In Me Two Worlds' doesn't appear in this anthology, you might find it helpful later to locate it in the *Collected Poems*. I'd like us to look now at 'The Conflict' (p. 199), thinking about the implications of the title. What is the nature of the conflict? And what hope, if any, does the poet hold out for its resolution?

DISCUSSION

The first three stanzas enlarge upon the poet's 'singing' in the face of potential disaster. How do you understand this? When a poet speaks of singing, he is likely to have in mind his own creative activities, and I think this is the case here, though we shouldn't allow this interpretation to preclude a more general sense of the speaker's defiance of a threatening future. Is that defiance heroic or merely evasive? You'll probably be familiar with the phrase 'to fiddle while Rome burns' – that is, to turn to the trivial while the forces of destruction rage about you; but I think you'll agree that Day Lewis' view of his own 'singing' is less negative than this.

There is, to begin with, that reference to the song's reinforcement of courage: the impending wave threatens to obliterate both light and life (the cutting off of the sun can be understood both figuratively and more or less literally) but even in the shadow of destruction we may find ourselves heroically able to assert our own vitality. The second stanza invokes the storm-cock, or misselthrush, a bird whose popular name refers to its habit of singing in the face of rough weather. You may be reminded of Thomas Hardy's poem 'The Darkling Thrush', with its dual suggestion of a threatening nightfall and the bird's illogical but inspiring denial of closure: the word 'carol' seems to echo Hardy's 'carollings', and the whole stanza offers similar suggestions of a stance at once affirmative and vulnerable. The image of the bird then gives place to the motif, recurrent in the 1930s and later to be given a more extended treatment by Day Lewis himself in a long poem entitled 'A Time to Dance', of the beleaguered yet heroic airman. The reference to the airman's clinging to the 'last drop of spirit' suggests not merely the aircraft's fuel but the driving energy behind human heroism.

Admirable as it may be, however, such heroism is ultimately inadequate: it takes place in isolation – 'Above the clouds, outside the ring' – and even induces an incongruous sense of 'peace'; the hero is both compromised and endangered by his failure to engage with the struggle between the two 'massing powers'. Innocence and privacy are no longer appropriate in a universe characterized by conflict.

You may have known that Day Lewis was a member of the Communist Party of Great Britain from 1935 to 1938, and a Communist sympathizer for some time before that; but even if not, you'll probably pick up on the significance of the phrase 'the red advance of life'. Relatable both to the 'blood-red dawn' which obliterates the stars of the singer's insular world and to the 'common blood' of mass endeavour, it serves to define the nature of the conflict: to invoke the colour of the Communist flag in a context such as this was a means – sometimes employed with considerably less subtlety than it is here – of displaying allegiance to the socialist cause. If, as I think we must, we understand the 'two massing powers' to be socialism on the one hand and, on the other, those forces inimical to a socialist world, there is little doubt as to where Day Lewis' sympathies lie.

Yet we oversimplify the poem if we regard the conflict of the title simply as one between opposing political factions. We need to return to Day Lewis' assertion that this is a poem 'of the divided mind'; to understand that the conflict is played out not only on the political stage, but also inwardly. Like many of his contemporaries, Day Lewis is concerned with the tension between the desire for privacy and the perceived need for forms of social engagement which demand the assumption of an active, public role. It is significant that his involvement with the Communist Party came to an end when, after having given an eloquent speech to a packed public meeting, he 'distinctly heard above the applause a small voice saying three or four times inside my head, "It won't do. It just won't do" '; he had, as he puts it, 'become sick of myself as a public figure and wished only to retire into a private life and write poetry'[2] – in other words, to reverse the procedure recommended in 'The Conflict' some five years earlier.

Day Lewis described the conclusion of this poem as 'a confident statement of the choice made'.[3] Do you agree? I wonder whether you feel, as I do, that the exhortation to 'move with new desires', while possibly addressed to others from a position of apparent certainty, might equally well be interpreted as the poet's urging himself towards a path which he has yet to take. Nevertheless, many of Day Lewis' political poems do read, on first acquaintance at least, like the confident statements of a man who has found his way in life: look, for example, at the brash opening lines of *The Magnetic Mountain* 20 (p. 63), in which the speaker berates those who, lacking his own political insight, allow themselves to be seduced and betrayed by a corrupt press. Aggressively rhetorical, strongly tendentious, this is an overtly propagandist piece of writing; you may wish to consider, as you read it, whether its unsophisticated bluntness constitutes a strength or a weakness.

DISCUSSION

Day Lewis begins, in approved oratorical fashion, with a direct acknowledgement of his audience: reading the opening lines, one can imagine him physically leaning forward from the public platform from which, by his own account, he was able to speak so eloquently. The alliterative list ('Fireman and farmer, father and flapper') is clearly not intended to exclude other categories of listener but, rather, to emphasize the immediacy of the speaker's relationship with his audience: 'I'm speaking to you,' he insists. You may be struck, however, by the implied inequality of the relationship; the hectoring tone is that of a teacher addressing a group of stupid or unenlightened pupils. You'll probably be unsurprised to learn that Day Lewis was indeed, at the time of writing *The Magnetic Mountain*, a schoolmaster.

We should perhaps think for a moment about the object of

Day Lewis' attack. The popular press was widely perceived in the 1930s as buttressing the more reactionary elements of British society; then, as now, certain newspapers were vilified in some quarters for pandering to the desires of a public hungrier for superficial sensationalism than for the kind of news which might provoke serious, and therefore potentially subversive, thought. The newspaper proprietors Beaverbrook (the 'Bimbo' of this poem) and Rothermere were the focus of considerable animosity: in his 'Letter to a Young Revolutionary', published in the same year as this poem, Day Lewis argued against throwing a bomb at 'Lords B[eaverbrook] and R[othermere]', not on the grounds that such violence was unacceptable, but simply because 'like other poisonous reptiles, they would live in their *disjecta membra* and we'd have twenty wriggling horrors instead of two'.[4] A year earlier, in *The Orators*, Auden had published a similar attack on 'Beethameer' (a barely disguised conflation of Beaverbrook and Rothermere) characterizing his target as the 'bully of Britain' and threatening to 'give you the thrashing you richly deserve'.

Fantasies of violence against representatives of the establishment were recurrent in the writings of the period, and Day Lewis' suggestion that he and his fellows are 'learning to shoot' represents a thinly veiled threat, though not one which a perceptive reader is likely to take either literally or seriously; I see the poem as an example of the 'bluster' which the poet explicitly attributes to the enemy. Day Lewis himself later recognized 'the shrill schoolboyish derisiveness which served for satire' in the bulk of his political verse;[5] does the phrase seem apt to this particular poem?

We might usefully ask ourselves the same question about *The Magnetic Mountain* 25 (p. 61). As so often in Day Lewis' poetry, the influence of Auden is apparent here. It's not the opening phrase alone which recalls Auden's 'Consider this and in our time'; the catalogue of doomed miscreants, while lacking its model's subtlety and variety, closely parallels the final stanza of Auden's poem. Again one recognizes the schoolmasterly tone; or perhaps even, in the crude pulpit oratory of lines such as 'Getters not begetters; gainers not beginners/Whiners, no winners; no triers, betrayers', or the threateningly resonant 'They that take the bribe shall perish by the bribe,' the accents of the hellfire preacher.

Day Lewis was in fact the son of a Church of Ireland clergyman; and he was, moreover, eventually to acknowledge explicitly the 'religious quality' of his political commitment during the 1930s.[6] He was by no means unique in this; speaking generally of contemporary political trends, Percy Wyndham Lewis observed in 1934 that 'it is definitely upon an intolerant religious impulse, of considerable virulence, that Marxism is floated and given momentum'.[7] Wyndham Lewis was an unfashionably right-wing thinker with his own axe to grind but, looking back at the two poems we've just examined, you may well feel that they help to substantiate his charge. A similar point was made with equal acerbity by a writer whose political sympathies were much closer to those of C. Day Lewis, the poet Julian Bell. In order to describe the attitude of what he termed 'the hot Marxians', Bell called to his service the words 'intolerance, violence, emotionalism and unreasonableness, and also mysticism and the search for salvation and a saviour'.[8] The context of that criticism gives it a particular significance here; it appeared in an open letter addressed to C. Day Lewis.

The 'search for salvation and a saviour' is well exemplified in *The Magnetic Mountain* 24, which begins with a series of images reminiscent of those in 'The Conflict', images of beleaguered heroism. In the penultimate stanza, however, the tone modulates from the assertive to the supplicatory: 'Father who endest all,/Pity our broken sleep' is a prayer, an address to a superior directive power. And the final stanza adumbrates an offering, a blood-sacrifice made for the sake of one explicitly referred to as a 'saviour'.

Religious imagery of this kind is recurrent in the sequence as a whole. The magnetic mountain of the title is characterized as 'miraculous', and it is perhaps significant that it is located 'Somewhere beyond the railheads/Of reason' (*The Magnetic Mountain* 3); it is attainable, that is, not by the exercise of the rational mind but, by implication, through faith. With these ideas in mind, I'd like us to turn now to *The Magnetic Mountain* 32 (p. 49).

DISCUSSION

The poem opens with the rhetorical flourish with which we're now becoming familiar: Day Lewis makes a direct play for his audience's attention (the opening 'You' is to recur at the beginning of each of the three succeeding stanzas) before going on to evoke the beauties of an essentially rural England. How do you respond to the musical analogies by means of which he builds up his picture? As so often with Day Lewis' writing, I find something mechanical about the process: the punning 'slow movement', the 'arias', 'chords', 'counterpoint', 'allegro', and the 'storms of wood strings brass' seem to me to have been applied as surface decoration rather than to have evolved as an organic feature of the verse; only the 'new theme' seems integral to the poem as a whole.

But what is the new theme? Like the 'new world' which crops

up twice here, like the 'new continent' and the 'new route' in Day
Lewis' earlier sequence *From Feathers to Iron*, the phrase seems
remarkably unspecific. It isn't, of course, the business of the poet
to provide specific remedies for social and psychological ills,
but I wonder if you share my view that there's something slightly
suspect about the vagueness of such phrases; the significantly
withheld offer to 'tell you a secret' is the utterance of a child
laying claim to knowledge more substantial than that which he
actually possesses.

You'll notice that in this poem Day Lewis refers not only to a
saviour but to an angelic presence – 'the visiting angel, the strange
new healer'; salvation seems to be dependent upon submission to
this heavenly visitor, upon an act of apparently unquestioning
faith in an externally located directive power. If you know something
of Marxist theory, you may find yourself objecting that such a
vision has nothing to do with Communism, but simply reflects
Day Lewis' inability to jettison the images and ideas appropriate
to his own Christian upbringing. I think this is largely true; yet the
Marxist concept of historical necessity – the idea, touched on in
the opening chapter, that individuals and societies are driven along
by largely uncontrollable historical forces – might well have served
to buttress visions of this kind. When, in poem XII of *From
Feathers to Iron*, Day Lewis wrote that 'Our wheels whirling with
impetus elsewhere/Generated we run, are ruled by rails', he may
well have been alluding, more or less directly, to these historical
forces; but you'll appreciate how close such an acknowledgement
may have brought him to the submissive gesture recommended in
The Magnetic Mountain 32.

The poem's final stanza moves through suggestions of degeneracy to a vision of renewed power. In his autobiography, Day
Lewis speaks of his 'susceptibility to the heroic', and this quality is
evident here as he closes his peroration with what is, in effect, a
ringing call to arms. Again, however, it seems to me that the
rhetoric half conceals, yet half exposes, a certain hollowness at the
poem's core; there's little here to make us query Day Lewis' later
misgivings about his political verse.

I would, however, want to make a case for 'Newsreel' (p. 69),
which Day Lewis doesn't place alongside 'The Conflict' and 'In
Me Two Worlds', yet which seems to me to be of comparable
quality and which is clearly, in the broad sense of the term, a
political poem. It takes up a theme touched on in *The Magnetic
Mountain* 20: the tendency of an inert public to insulate itself
from a threatening world. Please read it now.

DISCUSSION

The 'dream-house' of the first line is, of course, the cinema. As
A. J. P. Taylor has pointed out, the cinema was 'the essential
social habit of the age',[9] a force which 'took people from their
homes' and 'eclipsed both church and public house'.[10] Taylor's
observation that it was also 'the greatest educative force of the
early twentieth century'[11] needs to be set against a widespread
perception among intellectuals that it actually functioned as a
narcotic, stifling rather than stimulating the critical powers of its
audience; and Day Lewis clearly envisages it here as the equivalent
of an opium-den, a place of refuge from the insistent pressures of
the everyday world. The 'debts' and the 'history' which are left
behind on entry can be interpreted quite narrowly as the money
owed by, and the personal background of, each individual; but
as the poem unfolds we shall become aware that the responsibilities
which these people are evading are actually far greater than this.

You may find some difficulty in deciding whether those described in the second stanza – 'Clerk, spy, nurse, killer, prince, the
great and the defeated' – are figures from feature films or from the
newsreel of the title. The confusion may be deliberate and is
certainly appropriate: Day Lewis will go on to suggest that the
audience is itself dangerously incapable of distinguishing between
fantasy and reality, and 'incurious' about the relationship between
the two.

Like the newspaper readers in *The Magnetic Mountain* 20,
the cinemagoers are being supplied with 'dope' by a manipulative
establishment: images of careless frivolity are followed by that of
a politician enjoying his leisure hours. You'll recognize immediately
the irony of the suggestion that this last image proves that 'all is
well': that all is most emphatically not well has already been
implied by the disturbing reference in the preceding stanza to the
'furious/Sick shapes and pregnant fancies of your world'; and Day
Lewis now goes on to reinforce the point, focusing on a newsreel
image of military activity. The warplanes are manifestations of the
threatening world beyond the walls of the 'dream-house', and we
are clearly not intended to take at face value the suggestion that
the cinema audience, snugly cocooned in its comfortable darkness,
has no need to trouble itself about that world.

As the poem moves to its disquieting climax, Day Lewis'
ironies give way to a more direct assault. The guns bespeak man's
perversion of nature, implanting not life but death in the womb of
the world; the 'iron seed', literally the shells from the guns, com-

prehends the idea of semen (there's a particular brutality about the close juxtaposition of this hard image with that of the vulnerably 'soft' womb) and the product of the plant whose 'fire-bud, smoke-blossom' are representations of the visual manifestations of gunfire. With the botanic imagery to the fore, the poet now rounds on his audience with a question clearly intended to disturb its complacency. An exotic, in a botanical context, is a plant which originates in another country; in popular usage the term often also implies an inability to acclimatize. But Day Lewis' point, powerfully driven home in the final stanza, is that the horrors imaged on the screen will not be confined to their place of origin, but will spread to involve the insular, but by no means unassailable, world of those who refuse to acknowledge reality.

Like poems 20, 25 and 32 of *The Magnetic Mountain*, 'Newsreel' approaches its audience with an assertive directness, but the tone seems altogether more controlled. It's perhaps significant that Day Lewis addresses the cinema-goers as 'brothers and sisters', thereby reducing the effect of schoolmasterly or preacherly superiority. I think you'll agree, too, that it's a rather more complex and subtle poem than any we've looked at so far, not excluding 'The Conflict'. You might perhaps have picked up on the representation of the cinema's darkness as 'a fur you can afford', the phrase suggesting not merely the audience's desire for insulation from the rigours of the outside world but also a degree of identification with the luxuriously dressed heroines of the screen; you may also have made a connection back to those furs from the 'rags' of the final stanza—the horrific 'rags of children', which suggests torn flesh as well as tattered fabric. Or you may have noticed the way in which Day Lewis prepares us for the phallic imagery of the penultimate stanza, firstly through reference to the 'pregnant fancies' which, coloured by their proximity to the 'sick shapes', can only be interpreted negatively, as suggestive of monstrous rather than healthy procreation; and secondly through the phrase 'womb-deep sleep', which disturbingly reinforces the images of violation which follow. We can only regret that so few of Day Lewis' political poems attained this level of sophistication.

I don't imagine you'll have had any difficulty with the idea that 'Newsreel' is a political poem; but what about 'The Bells that Signed' (p. 85)? We're clearly a long way here from the overtly propagandist tendencies of *The Magnetic Mountain*, but you might nevertheless register the political overtones of this succinct representation of a diminished and degenerate world, perhaps making connection with the lines in *The Magnetic Mountain* 32 which describe those 'who have come to the far end, victims/Of a run-down machine'. Here, however, there is no 'visiting angel', no regenerative power: the bells of the poem's first stanza, no longer capable of setting their 'heavenly' seal on the rituals of society, are emblems of lost meaning.

The image of church- or cathedral-bells in the first stanza blends with that of the bell-buoy in the second. In practical terms the bell-buoy, warning of submerged dangers, may help to save lives; but the emphasis here is on 'What rots unfathomed in the dark', on the shadowy unwholesomeness signified by its presence. The final stanza reinforces the sense of loss: 'stone-lipped', particularly when read in conjunction with the 'iron hill' of the following line, may imply that the conqueror now exists only as a lifeless monument, or may simply be intended to suggest the sternness of his features; but there can be no doubt as to the implications of 'brood' and 'abject', or about the misery of the lovers who, unblessed by the bells, mourn a loss more far-reaching and damaging than that of their virginities.

Do you find that this poem, brief as it is, has an authority absent from those poems from *The Magnetic Mountain* which we examined earlier? That's certainly my feeling: in 'The Bells that Signed', Day Lewis provides no answers, no offers of salvation, but simply confronts the emptiness of an arguably degenerate age. As you'll already be aware from your reading, it was possible to respond more upliftingly to the pressures of the decade without writing dishonestly about them; but the best of Day Lewis' political poetry seems to me to be that in which his essentially pessimistic vision of society is not glibly countered with spurious suggestions of healing and rebirth, but acknowledged for what it is.

It may seem to you that my criticism of some of these poems has been rather harsh – though no harsher than Day Lewis' own retrospective judgement – and it's perhaps important to re-emphasize here the necessity of making your own evaluation. I would add that, despite certain reservations about its quality, I see Day Lewis' poetry as exemplifying with particular clarity tendencies characteristic of the period as a whole and believe that, on these grounds at least, it merits close and careful attention.

6. Observations: Geoffrey Grigson, Bernard Spencer, Kenneth Allott

We've already looked in some detail at the work of four poets who held, and continue to hold, a prominent place in the popular view of the decade and its literature. As we move on to examine the poetry of some of their less widely known contemporaries, it's worth bearing in mind the need to approach each poem openly and without undue regard to the supposed status of its author within a questionable literary hierarchy. Your responses to the poems which follow are unlikely, of course, to correspond exactly to mine; but I'd be surprised if, on a close and unprejudiced reading, you didn't feel that a number of them were equal or superior in quality to some of the poems discussed in previous chapters.

Geoffrey Grigson

Geoffrey Grigson was described by his slightly younger contemporary, Francis Scarfe, as a 'miniaturist', and his early poems certainly suggest a relish for detail, depicting, for example, 'the beetle/Shoving a clay ball up the shale' ('Incidents of Health'), 'the blue lungwort in the angle of the wall' ('The Night Sky') or 'the ringed wasp quivering in the rind' of fallen fruit ('Yes and No'). But we shouldn't assume that this delight in the meticulous delineation of the natural world represents a form of escapism:

Grigson, who travelled extensively in Europe in the years immediately preceding the outbreak of war, and who suggested that literature should comment as nearly as possible upon 'the whole of human activity',[1] was acutely aware of the wider social and political context of his poetry; and many of the poems he wrote during the 1930s reveal, directly or obliquely, his sense of living in a world charged with anxiety and unrest.

'And Forgetful of Europe' (p. 125) perfectly exemplifies both Grigson's 'miniaturism' and his wider understanding. The poem opens with the injunction to 'Think now ...', perhaps recalling Auden's minatory opening gambits, 'Consider this and in our time ...' or 'Look, stranger ...', though as it progresses we become aware that it is addressed in part to a specific individual ('my darling') who has actually shared with the poet the experience now being imaginatively recreated. Grigson's depiction of 'the things which made up/That place' is sharp-edged and colourful; the imagination at work here is primarily a visual one (you might register the uncharacteristic note of uncertainty which creeps in as he attempts to recollect the auditory impression of the 'doves/ Sounding among the figs') and as you read the poem through, it might strike you how readily it could be realized in cinematic terms. From the long shot which takes in canoes, peppers and figs under the plane tree, we home in on the Countess and ('as we came close') pick up on intimate physical detail; or we track up the flowered path to the orchard and the lucent stream, noting the precision with which Grigson – a keen and knowledgeable botanist – details the plant species en route.

The sharpness of the poet's eye is apparent throughout; but as we move towards the conclusion we become aware of the poem's deeper resonances. The edgy drumming of the Countess' varnished nails, the loss of money (perhaps prefiguring more significant losses) and the travellers' regret at the absence of a moon to light their homeward walk, all subtly compromise the idyll; and with the recurrence of the title-phrase, 'And forgetful of Europe', we recognize the shadowy background to the poem's luminous landscapes. As in other poems of the period, 'Europe' is being used here to signify that social and political disturbance which was widely recognized as the prelude to full-scale war; and Grigson's two prominent references to his earlier forgetfulness actually constitute a troubled recollection of the inescapable presence of violence and disorder. He was later to remark in his autobiography that 'enjoyment in these [pre-war] years was haunted by the spooks of Europe';[2] it's a statement which neatly illuminates the tension at the heart of this poem.

The same tension informs 'The Non-Interveners' (p. 142), though here enjoyment is far more oppressively shadowed by Grigson's sombre vision of political events in Europe. 'Non-intervention' had a specific meaning in 1937, the year of this poem's composition: it refers to the policy, favoured by Baldwin's National government, of standing aloof from the armed struggle in Spain. The policy was deeply unpopular with many British intellectuals, and Grigson's distaste is immediately apparent in his opening description of two non-interventionist politicians. We don't need to identify the two Ministers in question (they may indeed be imaginary) in order to understand that Grigson, like so many political satirists before and since, is highlighting selected physical detail as a means of suggesting moral degeneracy. The hand-someness of the first Minister is immediately qualified by the reference to his 'second/and a half chin' (indicative perhaps of luxurious living) and this is followed by an oblique hint, imprecise but suggestive, of intellectual inadequacy to his responsibilities: Grigson envisages a mind as small and as merely ornamental as a charm on a chain; the additional suggestion of 'heart-shaped', that the Minister's pursuits may be amatory rather than intellectual, compounds the criticism. The other Minister, with his stemlike neck, is physically diseased; gout was traditionally linked with what the eighteenth-century poet William Cowper, speaking of the ailment in his long poem 'The Task', calls 'libertine excess'. Images of bodily disease are frequently associated in the poetry of the 1930s – as indeed in the literature of many other periods – with an ineffectual or corrupt political system; you might like to look for yourselves, in this connection, at Roy Fuller's 'End of a City' (p. 255), a sustained account, with evident contemporary relevance, of the disintegration of a city presided over by a filthy, dropsical god.

Grigson then turns, with a characteristically abrupt shift of focus, from England to Spain; not, at first, to the horrors of the Civil War, but to the traditional Spain beloved of the tourist, with its striking architecture and scenery; the description at this point recalls that of the landscapes in 'And Forgetful of Europe'. But the tone then modulates through the subdued suggestion of death in 'the cuttle speared/at night' to something more sinister as Grigson speaks of the violence perpetrated by man against his fellows in the contemporary context of a bitter civil war. The 'black slime', which on first reading you may quite legitimately have referred back to the inky discharge of the speared cuttlefish, proves to be the blood of those shot, presumably executed, against a 'bullet-pocked wall'. Still more disturbingly, the poet goes on to speak of the blood-letting itself, of 'arterial blood/squirting into the curious future'. The image functions both as a shocking reminder of the physical brutality of war ('squirting' seems to me at once repugnant and clinically apt) and as a metaphor: Grigson is suggesting, accurately as it transpired, that the bloodshed in Spain is the prelude to further violence. The blood-imagery is subtly sustained in a further reference to the violence of war: the 'greasy cloud streaked with red in yellow' is primarily suggestive of fire or explosion, but it may also seem to you to recall, through the adjective 'greasy', the 'black slime' of the first reference to blood; while the phrase 'streaked with red' is clearly relatable to the two preceding images.

The final section of the poem turns again to England; but whereas the initial movement from England to Spain was some-what abruptly effected, Grigson now suggests, by the use of the conjunction 'and' which bridges the second and final sections, a relationship between the two countries, a community of concern which may be implicitly denied by the 'indifferent headline' but which is clearly central to the poet's vision. You'll notice that, despite the indifference of its headline and the implied inadequacy of its correspondent's coverage of events, the newspaper is described as 'ominous', the adjective picking up on the earlier suggestion of a violent and bloody future. The poem's concluding lines, remin-iscent of the description of the Spanish scenery which subsequently shaded so disturbingly into images of bloodshed, represent an economically delineated portrait of a land under threat from forces it unwisely chooses to ignore.

How successfully do you feel Grigson has addressed con-temporary issues in these two poems? You may be tempted to argue that, while the broadly political theme of 'The Non-Interveners' is clearly integral to the poem, acknowledgement of the wider political context is, in a structural sense at least, marginal to 'And Forgetful of Europe': lose the title and final two lines of the latter and you're left with a brilliant and sharply realized travelogue, superficially attractive but decidedly limited in per-spective. It's worth bearing in mind, however, that forgetfulness is the theme of this poem: the poet's narrow focus forces us to enact his temporary obliviousness; and you may feel, as I do, that the very limited reference to Europe in its broader sense actually represents not an artistically suspect omission but a finely judged strategy for involving us in the experiences both of forgetting and remembering.

You may find it more difficult to relate 'Three Evils' (p. 223) to its historical context, and Skelton's placing of it under the heading 'When Logics Die' seems rather unhelpful in this respect. In fact, it's an essentially logical and coherent poem which shares with 'The Non-Interveners' its pronounced sense of present unwholesomeness and impending danger; and though its connection with contemporary events is clearly less specific, it nevertheless reflects something of Grigson's undoubted sensitivity to the prevailing political climate.

Grigson's positioning of the adjective 'ominous' at the end of the first line, detached from its noun in a way which obliges us to linger over it as we read, gives it a particular prominence; and, as in 'The Non-Interveners', the word resonates throughout the poem as a whole. 'Ominous' means, of course, related to omens and the foretelling of future events; in the past the word could be used neutrally or even positively (some omens, after all, presage good fortune) but current usage is all but restricted to the idea of a threatening future, and this is clearly Grigson's emphasis here. The colour of the sky suggests storm clouds, a traditional image of impending disaster; it's not irrelevant to note that the title of William Empson's 1940 collection of poems was *The Gathering Storm*, and that the same phrase crops up again as the title of that volume of Sir Winston Churchill's history of the Second World War which deals largely with the period immediately preceding its outbreak. Comparison of the lowering sky with a bruise has the further effect of evoking those ideas of brutality and violence which figure more obviously, though not necessarily more significantly, in 'The Non-Interveners'.

Although the skyward glance seems to disclose imminent danger, Grigson urges us to concern ourselves less with 'the spirits from the sky/Than the spirits from the earth'. The suggestion is that, whatever the future may hold, the evil represented by the spirits is already with us; the phrase 'under your feet' implies immediacy as well as obstruction. Reference to their habitat (the unclean connotations of lavatories and leaked oil are obvious) reinforces our sense of the spirits' essential nastiness. You may not have come across henbane, now a rather uncommon plant, but you'll probably be aware that 'bane' means 'poison'; more than a century earlier another botanizing poet, George Crabbe, had described 'the henbane's faded green/And pencilled flower of sickly scent' in his long poem, *The Borough*, appropriately locating the plant in an environment of filth and squalor among the dwellings of the outcast poor.

Grigson then moves via the invalid, a figure emblematic of sickness and shabbiness, to contemplation of what he describes as the worst of the three evils, 'the Sybil,/The rare Marocaine' (a Marocaine is a female native of Morocco). She is, like the spirits of the earth and the invalid, a present evil; but in characterizing her Grigson comes full circle, gesturing outward once again to the insistent and disturbing future. The Sibyls (usually so spelt, though the spelling given here is one of a number of variants) were Greek prophetesses, the most celebrated of whom was the Cumaean Sibyl; if you know T. S. Eliot's 'The Waste Land' – another poem much concerned with prognostication of a disquieting future – you'll doubtless remember the reference to her in the poem's epigraph. Here, Grigson goes on to refer explicitly to the prophetic role of his contemporary Sibyl; like other legendary figures, she consults a revelatory mirror, in this case one composed of tar. This last detail may remind you of the oil patches in the second stanza, and certainly serves to suggest the sinister nature of the Sibyl's foreknowledge; such light as is implied in the idea of reflection is alarmingly qualified by the profound darkness of the tar itself.

I don't believe that we should interpret this poem in narrowly socio-political terms, reading it simply as a precognitive vision of impending war; its frame of reference is clearly broader than this, and we shall betray its complexity and subtlety if we attempt too exclusive a definition of its meaning. But reading it through, particularly in conjunction with 'And Forgetful of Europe' and 'The Non-Interveners', you may well feel that, while susceptible of more general as well as more personal interpretations, this is nevertheless a poem deeply informed by the imminence of war; it certainly strikes me as an excellent example of the way in which a poem may reflect, without directly addressing, the social and political concerns of its author.

Bernard Spencer

The writing of poetry was only one aspect of Grigson's remarkable range of literary activity; he was perhaps best known during the 1930s as the fierce and perceptive editor of *New Verse*, arguably the finest and most influential of the small literary periodicals which came into being during the decade. Both Bernard Spencer and Kenneth Allott were closely associated with *New Verse*, initially as contributors and latterly as assistant editors; and Allott was later to refer (in the introduction to his *Penguin Book of Contemporary Verse*) to Spencer's 'Allotments' as representative of 'the kind of poem for which *New Verse* stood: straightforward but unpedestrian language, feeling expressed through observation, intelligence reflecting on observation and awake to the implications

of feeling'. This seems to me to be at once a fair assessment of
the virtues of *New Verse* and an accurate account of Spencer's
'Allotments' (p. 105); perhaps you'd like to read the poem through
now, with Allott's words in mind, and see how far you agree with
his estimation of it.

The poem, which deals with the return of Spring, belongs to a
long tradition of celebratory verse; but you'll see at once that the
celebratory impulse is hedged around by caution and uncertainty.
The very title implies a suggestive combination of growth and
circumscription: allotments are small parcels of land usually
apportioned to town-dwellers for the growing of vegetables; if the
term here evokes ideas of seed-time and potential harvest, it also
hints at a world of diminished perspectives. The adjective 'squared'
in the second line reinforces this reading; and even 'rings' in the
first line, though probably referring primarily to the sound of the
writer's footsteps against the stone, contributes to the impression
of enclosure.

The guarded, equivocal note is sustained as Spencer continues:
'hallooing' and 'rousing' certainly suggest vigour and vitality, but
these qualities are located with the season; the poet himself, eyes
dazzled by the sunlight, stands a little apart, openly questioning
the extent of his own participation in the regenerative processes he
describes. His response to his own question embodies the concepts
of joy, resurrection and renewal, but qualifies these in advance
with the positionally dominant phrase 'lost to some of us'; the
traditional rituals of spring are not, he suggests, in the profoundest
sense accessible to him or to those of his contemporaries whose
lives are similarly constructed on doubt rather than on faith. Nor
can he find any simple answer in the erotic love so frequently
associated with spring: you'll probably recognize the quotation
'the only pretty ring-time' as a phrase from the light-hearted song
sung by the banished duke's pages in Shakespeare's *As You Like
It*, and you'll doubtless understand (though you may wish to
disagree with its implied inclusiveness) the suggestion that the
love-lyrics of the middle ages and Renaissance are inadequate to
convey the urgent and predatory nature of a passion notable for
its destructive powers.

Although largely concerned with those joys which the season
does *not* offer the poet, the second and third stanzas each conclude
with a less negative definition: the religious dimension may be
lacking or attenuated, sexual love may manifest itself in savage
and disruptive forms, but Spencer can still relish the concrete
detail of his immediate surroundings. Even this modest pleasure,
however, is subject to further qualification as he takes us from

contemplation of such detail to an acknowledgement of cir-
cumstantial violence. The beet-leaves and flower-pots are described
as making 'a pause in/The wireless voices repeating pacts, persecutions,/And imprisonments and deaths and heaped violent
deaths', but they have in fact generated these references to their
own disturbing context: like Grigson's speared cuttlefish in 'The
Non-Interveners' the 'veins' and 'fires' function as links with more
threatening areas of experience. If you have any doubt about this,
look at the recurrence of the word 'heaped' in the penultimate line
of the fourth stanza: its first appearance, two lines earlier, may
initially have seemed innocently descriptive of the way in which
the pots have been stacked against the hut-walls; but its second
appearance, in explicit association with the concept of violent
death, affects our response to the earlier image, so that it becomes
difficult or impossible to dissociate the stacked pots from the
victims of violence in the world beyond. The point is clear: our
homely perspectives, our personal lives, cannot legitimately be
separated from our wider responsibilities; and Spencer moves on,
via recognition of the sombre presence of the town and the urban
poor, to a vision of inclusiveness, implicitly rejecting denial and
concealment in favour of a more accommodating approach. It is
of course, strictly speaking, the season which 'does not deny or
conceal' and the elms which, in the poem's final line, adopt a
'balanced attitude'; but these references to assimilation and equi-
librium are clearly part of the poet's attempt to answer the question
which forms the title of another of his poems: 'How must we
live?'

Such questions crop up again and again in Spencer's work
as, indeed, throughout the decade's poetry as a whole. Look,
for example, at the structure of 'Evasions' (p. 183), the bulk of
which is in question form. The questions themselves centre on the
individual's relationship with his fellows, each embodying an
implicit criticism of the present nature of that relationship. The
suggestions of hypocrisy in the first stanza and, in the second and
third, of lack of engagement in both private and public domains,
are plain enough: humouring those who deserve criticism, refusing
to accept the deeper ties of sexual love or the wider ones of social
responsibility, clearly constitute forms of evasion. Perhaps the
most reprehensible of evasions, however, is that which meets these
searching and important questions with a brusque, formulaic dismissal: the last line of each stanza represents a reinstatement of
the self-protective enclosure threatened by enquiry.

While Spencer clearly regards such evasions as unacceptable,
his criticism is subdued and oblique, suggestive rather than con-

frontative; and this is perhaps in part attributable to his recognition that the desire for self-enclosure is one aspect of his own complex response to the world's insistent demands. The inherent contradictions of that response form the focus of 'A Cold Night' (p. 143), a poem in which images of insularity and warmth are repeatedly challenged by counter-suggestions of a cold and disruptive pressure from outside. It is, indeed, the wider context which is given prominence by the poem's title; and the first two lines set up a pattern for the poem as a whole, the comforting associations of 'thick wool' being immediately subverted by suggestions of the fabric's inadequacy against a cold and penetrating wind.

As you read on, you'll quickly recognize the poem's fundamental self-contradiction: if it's true that the world is 'lopped' at the radius of the poet's fire – in other words, that his own narrowly delineated sphere of warmth and privacy excludes the wider world – then why the insistence on the bitter wind and the trembling shop-boys? 'Only for a moment', says Spencer, turning outward once again to register the plight of other sufferers from the punishing weather and, by extension, the prevailing social and political climate; but it is precisely this purportedly fleeting apprehension of suffering beyond the firelit enclosure which dominates the poem. The depiction of the newspaper sellers and whores, emblems of the poverty and degradation which he locates in the world beyond his doors, paradoxically possesses an immediacy lacking from the poet's reference to his domestic surroundings; even the 'soldiery', undifferentiated victims and perpetrators of violence in distant Spain, are more sharply realized than the features of the room he occupies.

Spencer's recollection of his own earlier experience of that same bitter wind represents a further subversion of the suggestion of privacy. It's not simply a question of his sharing the experience with others, though this is important and is arguably reinforced by the image of the bridge, to which we may want to assign a figurative as well as a literal meaning; there is also a profound significance in that reference to the 'grill/Through which, instead of flames, wind hates'.

The poet's method here closely parallels that by which, in 'Allotments: April', he effects a link between the 'heaped' flower pots in the allotments and the 'heaped violent deaths' in the world beyond. The flames undoubtedly suggest destruction (the syntax associates them, as well as the wind, with hatred, and you may well find yourself relating them back to the image of war-torn Madrid at the beginning of the stanza) and once again Spencer seems to be emphasizing the connective threads which make escape impossible: he cannot subsequently 'turn back to [his] fire' without at the same time evoking the disquieting manifestations of fire in the outside world.

The poem's conclusion powerfully confirms these suggestions of an enclosure breached by forces it cannot repel; as the long final sentence develops, the poet's self-justificatory assertion of the individual's need for privacy and inward warmth is undermined by the very thing he explicitly resolves to forget. It is the cold insistence of 'winter, winter, like a hammering rhyme' which governs both the content and cadences of these closing lines; the insular comfort of the firelit room is defined by implication as both inappropriate and ultimately unattainable.

Kenneth Allott

Similar concerns inform the poetry of Kenneth Allott, the third of the poets I've selected for consideration in this chapter: in 'Christmas After Munich', for example, a poem written in 1938 shortly after Neville Chamberlain's last-ditch attempt to avert war with Germany, he contemplates the manifestations of crisis from the dubious security of the warm bedroom he shares with his lover, emphasizing the vulnerability of his insular state in the poem's final image of the clock's hands which 'move on to the dangerous morning'. Not all of Allott's work registers the pressure of external events as directly than this, but his poetry was clearly a means of grappling with the disturbing forces around him: although he argued in the celebrated 'Commitments' number of *New Verse* for a modest, localized perspective, maintaining that it was 'better to do something for your street, your suburb, your town, your county than to tremble like Keats or a leaf over the woes of continents or worlds,'[3] his poetry in fact turns repeatedly outward to the 'white continents' ('End of a Year') or the 'map of Europe in its coat of so many colours' ('Against the Clock'). 'Who,' he asks, 'can watch suffering Europe and not be angry?' ('Exodus'); the inescapable implication is that the poet is himself one of the troubled observers.

'Prize for Good Conduct' (p. 140) is a poem about war, and in particular about the waste and suffering it entails. Like Spencer, whose 'A Thousand Killed' (p. 141) concludes with an acknowledgement that the price of victory is 'the lives, burned-off,/Of young men and boys', Allott is concerned with the debris war leaves in its wake: any positive suggestion implicit in the statement that 'the War will soon be over' is quickly undercut as he creates a potent assemblage of images evocative of death, sacrilege, mutilation and neurosis; the poem's final lines hint at levels of evil which are in a literal or near-literal sense diabolical.

Although 'Prize for Good Conduct' seems to draw much of its material from the collective experience of the First World War, its strength actually lies partly in its lack of specificity. Despite the stark clarity of certain individual images, the poem as a whole is characterized by a suggestive vagueness which allows us to read it as prognostication as well as recollection, as a broadly significant vision of disorder rather than a strict delineation of historical events. You'll perhaps be struck, too, by the fragmentary nature of the imagery: look at the opening of the second stanza where, in spite of an internal logic of association, we can see quite clearly a form of disjunction which is in fact characteristic of Allott's poetry; in this particular case, the incomplete syntax and punctuation reinforce the effect. Allott later supplied commas at the end of the first and second lines of this stanza (this version is taken from *New Verse* where the poem was first published) but the added punctuation doesn't significantly modify the impression of imagistic fragmentation.

'Offering' (p. 213) reveals the same tendency with particular clarity. It's true that the act of offering functions as a kind of connective thread for the catalogue of images, but the overriding impression is not of connection but of separateness; the images appear to be related in the same way as a series of beads on a string, not organically but simply by the fact of their juxtaposition. This is not to deny the isolated power of some of these images: Roy Fuller, introducing Allott's *Collected Poems* in 1975, quoted from this poem as evidence of the poet's 'imaginative daring' the lines 'The withered arm of the last century/Cannot provoke a demon to anger us'; and you might feel, as I do, that the poem contains others still more striking.

You may also feel, however, that there's something rather unsatisfactory about this lengthy catalogue of offerings; that the poet's audacious imaginative leaps don't preclude, and may even be responsible for, a mechanically repetitive verbal and imagistic pattern. Like others of Allott's poems (look, for example, at 'Men Walk Upright' and 'Azrael' in the *Collected Poems*) it's structurally unsophisticated, a collection of fragments rather than an organically developed whole. It's perhaps worth noting that it first appeared in considerably shorter form in an Oxford periodical, under the title 'Poem: For K. L.'; yet the addition of five new stanzas doesn't fundamentally alter a poem whose cumulative structure readily accommodates such additions, as indeed (think how little damage would be effected by the removal of any one of the first seven stanzas) it largely tolerates excisions.

Allott's use of these relatively simple cumulative structures is by no means a merely personal idiosyncrasy; his catalogues are actually manifestations of a tendency widespread in the poetry of the period. We've already looked at poems by Geoffrey Grigson which clearly exemplify that tendency: Roy Fuller, in a contemporary review of Grigson's significantly titled first collection, *Several Observations*, was quick to point out that the objects of the poet's verse were 'mainly the objects of a catalogue';[4] and, while we might wish to pay tribute to the subtlety with which Grigson selects and orders his material, most of us would recognize the aptness of Fuller's remark to such poems as 'And Forgetful of Europe', 'The Non-Interveners' and 'Three Evils'. Bernard Spencer's poems may display the tendency in less obvious form, but it's certainly recognizable in both 'Allotments' and 'A Cold Night'; looking back on his poetry from the vantage point of the 1960s, Martin Dodsworth characterized Spencer as 'the poet of addition' and his work as representative of 'a poetry that accumulated detail in the present tense, adding clause to clause in a theoretically endless because arbitrarily related series'.[5]

As so often in dealing with general trends in the poetry of the 1930s, we're drawn back inexorably to the dominant figure of Auden. Referring in 1938 to 'Auden's notorious catalogues',[6] MacNeice implied that criticism of this feature of his fellow poet's work had by then become commonplace; and we can see the operation of the tendency from a very early stage in Auden's poetic development, for example in these lines from the 1928 verse drama 'Paid on Both Sides':

> The Spring unsettles sleeping partnerships,
> Foundries improve their casting process, shops
> Open a further wing on credit till
> The winter. In summer boys grow tall
> With running races on the froth-wet sand,
> War is declared there, here a treaty signed;
> Here a scrum breaks up like a bomb, there troops
> Deploy like birds.

You'll appreciate from our earlier discussion of Auden how influential such patterns might be, but simply to define as 'Audenesque' the catalogues of contemporaries such as Allott, Grigson and Spencer is of limited critical value, highlighting literary influence at the expense of those more profound pressures which might make a particular mode of expression appropriate: the widespread use of the catalogue can perhaps more usefully be read as a reflection of the uncertainty and indirection which we've already identified as broadly characteristic of this troubled generation. Where belief is strong, writing is likely to be tendentious, its objects used purposively (think, for example, of Milton's 'Paradise Lost' with its opening statement of intent and insistent 'argument', or Wordsworth's 'Prelude' where Nature's manifestations tend so strongly towards the formation of the poet's mind); conversely, where belief is weak and no firm ideological scheme dictates an argumentative or developmental structure, lists such as that provided by Allott's 'Offering' may seem particularly appropriate. I see in Allott's work generally a remarkable but often essentially undirected energy, and it's perhaps relevant to note that after the publication of his second collection, *The Ventriloquist's Doll*, his creative talent seems to have deserted him; it may be that the limited development of individual poems implied, or was implicit in, a more fundamental failure of poetic development.

Reviewing David Gascoyne's 1936 collection, *Man's Life is This Meat*, Allott remarked: 'What seems to me lacking is an urgency best but not necessarily derived from an attitude to experience.'[7] That last phrase is vague; but it may seem to you, as it does to me, that Allott's criticism locates in Gascoyne's poetry the very flaw which ultimately vitiates his own. You may like to bear in mind that criticism, as well as my suggestion of relationship, as we go on to examine Gascoyne's work in the next chapter.

7. Inner and Outer Worlds: David Gascoyne, Dylan Thomas

David Gascoyne

To describe David Gascoyne as the father of English literary Surrealism is not, perhaps, to make any very substantial claim: Surrealism, which had flourished in France and Spain since the publication of André Breton's *Manifesto of Surrealism* in 1924, was certainly acknowledged by many British writers during the middle years of the following decade, but largely failed to establish itself as a movement here; and Gascoyne's pre-eminence may seem a rather hollow distinction. He is, nevertheless, an interesting and sometimes impressive poet, whose own work in the 1930s was influenced by Continental Surrealist sources; and we need briefly to examine those sources as a prelude to discussion of individual poems.

Drawing significantly on what Breton termed 'the magnificent discoveries of Freud'[1] while at the same time registering the influence of such diverse literary figures as Blake, Coleridge, Lewis Carroll, Edward Lear and Arthur Rimbaud, Surrealism insisted on the primacy of the random, the irrational and the uncontrolled in art. Painters and writers alike created images suggestive of a rich, if disordered, imaginative world. You may well be familiar with the work of that most theatrical and successful of Surrealist artists, Salvador Dali, as well as with the subtler paintings of René

Magritte; their literary counterparts are less widely known, but you may have come across work by such writers as Paul Eluard, Benjamin Péret and Breton himself.

Breton's definition of Surrealism as 'thought's dictation, in the absence of all control exercised by the reason and outside all aesthetic or moral preoccupations'[2] is one which certainly characterizes the ostensible aims of the first wave of Surrealist art; but you may be wondering, even as you read it, whether an artist can actually sever his 'thought' so neatly from rational, aesthetic and moral considerations. In fact, the idea of Surrealism as a moral or even political force was never far from the surface, and emerged with increasing frequency as the movement developed. By 1931, a periodical entitled *Le Surrealisme au Service de la Revolution* [*Surrealism in the Service of the Revolution*] was explicitly aligning Surrealism with Soviet communism; still more significant was the endorsement by Breton himself, within the pages of the first issue, of the 'spiritual and moral position' taken up by the revolutionary Soviet poet, Maiakovsky. Gascoyne's own account of the movement, *A Short Survey of Surrealism*, doesn't foreground the contradiction, but its final chapter suggests that by 1935 Surrealism has moved on from 'pure psychic automatism' to assume a more active social and political role in the world at large.

Gascoyne's poem 'The Very Image' (p. 234) is dedicated to René Magritte and offers a verbal equivalent of the displaced or oddly juxtaposed images we find in the Surrealist painter's work. You'll see at once the structural relationship between this poem and Allott's 'Offering', discussed in the previous chapter: the phrase 'an image of' at the opening of each stanza but the last provides the same kind of excuse as Allott's 'I offer you' for the stringing together of a group of largely disparate images. The relative weakness of Gascoyne's poem doesn't, I think, stem from any kind of Surrealist excess but, on the contrary, from its imaginative tameness; the images prove on examination to be no more than superficially arresting, their juxtaposition bizarre, but too calculatedly so. The second stanza suggests with particular clarity how far we are in this poem from Breton's notion of uncontrolled thought; crow, chair and fir-tree are not, surely, the vital creations of an unfettered imagination but stage props neatly arranged (Gascoyne actually uses this word in the final stanza) for our perusal.

I'm much more impressed by 'And the Seventh Dream is the Dream of Isis' (p. 229), a poem whose insistent evocation of evil, disease, death and decay gives it a coherence belied by its fragmented surface. You'll probably know that the 'Isis' of the poem's title was one of the deities of ancient Egypt, but we may need to think a little about her possible relevance here. Particularly closely associated with funerary ritual, she would seem an appropriate figure to introduce – perhaps, as the title may suggest, to generate – the death-laden imagery of the poem. We might also recall the proverbial phrase 'to lift the veil of Isis', meaning to penetrate a profound mystery; this is, with all the mystical overtones of the term, a poem of revelation, a prophetic work in the Blakean tradition.

How can we usefully analyse the welter of images thrown up by this kind of writing? We might perhaps approach the poem from a broadly Freudian angle, focusing on the recurrent sexual imagery: the collocation of needles and hair-filled reservoirs, the tree-trunks which 'burst open to release streams of milk' and the illnesses given to 'possessors of pistols' might seem to the phallically orientated psycho-analytical mind to give as clear an indication of sexual obsession as the more overt references to children who 'offer themselves to unfrocked priests' or who 'stick photographs of genitals to the windows of their homes'. Such an approach might also pick up on the element of unease or even disgust which seems to surround such references, as well as on a markedly iconoclastic streak, which runs through the poem as a whole: by defacing the windows of their homes or offering themselves to those whose own contraventions have resulted in their expulsion from the Church, these sexually precocious juveniles (and by extension Gascoyne himself) are striking out at the conventional framework supplied by family, religion and the law.

But psycho-analytical speculation of this kind needs to be balanced by a sense of the text's wider significance: I would suggest that the poem reflects not merely a disturbed mind but a disturbed world, and that we need to think more broadly, acknowledging the poet's psychical individuality, certainly, but recognizing at the same time the pressure of external factors. Gascoyne had been influenced by his reading of Oswald Spengler's *The Decline of the West*, a work whose considerable popularity during the inter-war years was undoubtedly attributable to the fact that its apocalyptic message seemed at once to explain and to be endorsed by the social and political convulsions in Europe and beyond. One of Gascoyne's early poems, 'The New Isaiah', is dedicated to the German philosopher and envisages the collapse of a society of sinners who 'go a-whoring with their own inventions/ deaf to the cries of one who sees their fate'. By October 1934, Gascoyne was referring to himself as a 'poet with continually growing political convictions'[3] and dissociating himself explicitly

from Surrealism's more introspective tendencies. The psychological curiosities of 'And the Seventh Dream...', first published
exactly a year earlier, clearly don't preclude a sociopolitical
interpretation.

There can be no doubt of the breadth of vision which informs
Gascoyne's powerfully evocative valediction to the 1930s, 'Farewell
Chorus' (p. 283). Unlike the two Surrealist pieces we've just
looked at, this poem has a sophisticated developmental structure;
and the development is one which takes us from the local and
personal, through a widening perception of historical context, to
an essentially religious vision of transcendence. The immediate
setting of the poem is the railway carriage in which the poet
describes himself as being borne away from his home town and
towards the war which had been declared some four months
earlier. The emphasis at this stage is on mundane detail: the
'angry waiting and cold tea' which have preceded departure and
the 'wet hankies' of those bidding farewell to the travellers are
aspects of what might at first seem a fairly restricted view. But
these homely images are already preparing us for the poem's
wider perspectives: the tear-soaked handkerchiefs emblematize a
grief whose deeper resonances become apparent as the poem
proceeds, while the reference to the 'years' of waiting, which we
might initially interpret simply as petulant exaggeration on the
part of the speaker, offers a hint, later to be developed much more
fully, of the broader significance of the journey.

Much of the remainder of the first section of the poem is
taken up with a retrospective appraisal of personal relationships.
The emphasis is upon failure: the second stanza suggests those
relationships unable to progress beyond a certain point because of
inadequacies or reluctance on the part of the unspecified other or
others, while the third stanza delicately balances these suggestions
by highlighting the speaker's own evasion of the implicit demands
of those who have unavailingly wished for closer communion with
him; the fourth invokes those with whom contact has been too
fleeting to allow any development of relationship, yet who represent
unexplored possibilities. The tone here is one of nostalgia and
regret, the focus self-engrossedly personal: it's significant that the
speaker imagines himself not as having failed to make significant
contact with other individuals, but with 'lost selves'.

The 'Away, away!' of the section's final stanza indicates,
however, a shift of perspective: committed to the journey, alert to
broadening geographies, the speaker rejects the backward glance,
leaving 'no longer in retreat' but with his eye on a future 'frontier'
and the necessity of crossing it. The movement is away from a life

now characterized as inappropriately circumscribed, and into a wider world. The 'exhausted implications' (the noun's more literal suggestions of entanglement may come to mind here as we imagine the speaker struggling to free himself from his past) are to be replaced by 'unimpassioned recollection', while the 'small fears' are similarly obliterated by the speaker's changing circumstances and perceptions.

Ideas of extroversion and enlargement were recurrent in the poetry of the 1930s but, particularly in the early years of the decade, tended to reflect a somewhat facile optimism. John Lehmann's 'Calm as the Moon' is a particularly apposite example, concluding as it does with 'The thunder of engines in a glass-roofed terminus, /The advance out of shadow and the crowd of lifted arms'.[4] But Gascoyne's 'small fears' are to give way not to sunlight but to greater terrors: the poem's second section moves towards confrontation of a future defined in terms which directly recall the apocalyptic mood of 'And the Seventh Dream...'. The 'sphinx-face' of the coming decade may be, like that of Isis, veiled, but you're likely to be aware of the predatory nature of the riddling Greek Sphinx, and may also perhaps know of the disturbing presence of the man-headed Egyptian Sphinx in that most celebrated of modern prophetic poems, W. B. Yeats' 'The Second Coming'; the staring figure which Gascoyne imagines here is clearly an emblem of anticipated disaster.

The point is reinforced by the reference to the smashing of the glass – an image which immediately recalls the cataclysmic conclusion of 'And the Seventh Dream...' ('And the drums of the hospitals were broken like glass/and glass were the faces in the last looking-glass'). Although the image which 'Farewell Chorus' calls up for you is likely to be, in the first instance, of the shattering of the drinking-glass from which the speaker imagines taking his 'final' draught, you may also find yourselves entertaining the subsidiary image of a broken mirror (the 'looking-glass' of 'And the Seventh Dream...'). This would seem entirely appropriate: the proverbial notion of a coming period of misfortune, coupled with suggestions of the impossibility of continuing self-regard, contributes pertinently to the poem's symbolic freight.

By this stage in the poem, you'll probably have quite a strong sense of the symbolic significance of the journey: even without the direct reference to his travelling 'towards some Time-to-Come', it would be clear enough that the speaker sees himself not merely as a passenger journeying from his home town towards a distant destination, but as one borne through life on the wheels of history towards a threatening future. Partially concealed or suppressed during the 1930s, the 'dangerous truth', he suggests, must now be acknowledged: the West is in decline (Spengler is explicitly invoked in the final stanza of this section) and men are being drawn by forces beyond their control towards a disastrous end.

The poem's final section represents a further enlargement of vision, offering an essentially religious perspective on the world's tribulations. The 'lowering of the Western skies' is now counterbalanced by the image of 'a new light' which both irradiates and heals: the phrase 'clear as ice to our sore riddled eyes' suggests at once a clarification of vision and the soothing coolness which reduces inflammation. The punning 'riddled', besides reinforcing the suggestion of 'sore', returns us to the image of the veiled 'sphinx-face': the light, it is implied, will resolve hitherto unanswered questions.

Although the radiance is described as lighting 'our actual scene', its source is more distantly located: 'motionless and far', it leads the gaze 'into the nameless and unknown/Extremes of this existence', towards a reality which transcends the immediate loss and turmoil of 'our dereliction's vortex'. The references to the viaticum (the Eucharist as administered to a dying person) and to transfiguration (the word, though subsequently secularized, originally referring specifically to Christ's revelation of himself, as a source of light, to three of his disciples) emphasize the religious nature of a journey whose end is both acquiescence and affirmation: the transcendence, through acceptance, of the human condition.

I suggested in my earlier discussion of the poetry of C. Day Lewis that a largely unacknowledged religious impulse might underlie some of the political writing of the 1930s. Gascoyne's 'Farewell Chorus' differs significantly from the poems mentioned in that connection: overtly religious, moving with assurance from the mundane to the visionary, it impresses me as a remarkably mature achievement for a poet still only twenty-three years old at the time of its composition.

Dylan Thomas

Two years older than Gascoyne, Dylan Thomas was a similarly precocious writer: as his biographer, Paul Ferris, points out, Thomas had, by the age of twenty, written 'more than thirty, probably more than forty, of the ninety *Collected Poems* in their final or near-final versions'.[5] His work is often difficult; you may feel on reading some of the poems included in this anthology that your uncertainty as to their meaning is a barrier to enjoyment. If this is your response, it might be helpful to approach Thomas' poetry, in the first instance, in a spirit of open receptivity, enjoying its music and allowing its images to work on your mind. It's an approach which may seem unfashionably lacking in academic rigour, but it's one which Thomas' account of his own creative methods would suggest to be appropriate. Writing to Henry Treece in 1938, he argued that he did not write the kind of poem which 'moves around one idea, from one logical point to another' but that which

> needs a host of images, because its centre is a host of images. I make one image, – though 'make' is not the word, I let, perhaps, an image be 'made' emotionally in me and then apply to it what intellectual & critical forces I possess – let it breed another, let that image contradict the first, make, of the third image bred out of the other two together, a fourth contradictory image, and let them all, within my imposed formal limits, conflict.[6]

The suggestion is of a vision at once multiple and volatile; and it's arguable that narrow or rigid definitions of meaning may be particularly unhelpful in a case of this kind.

Thomas' account emphasizes fluidity, but doesn't imply the complete absence of authorial control: you'll appreciate the significance of his insistence on his own 'intellectual & critical forces' and the 'imposed formal limits' within which he works. If we turn to 'Light Breaks Where No Sun Shines' (p. 221) we'll notice at once the strictness of the metrical framework within which the images 'breed' and 'conflict'; it's clear that the imagery, however audacious, is in some sense governed by a taut and meticulous craftsmanship.

How do we interpret this poem? We might begin by noting an imagistic pattern which repeatedly draws connections between inner and outer worlds. Though the sun itself does not reach the inner world, there is light within – a point reinforced in the first lines of the third and fifth stanzas; though there is no sea, the tidal 'waters of the heart' hold sway there; man generates a fruit which 'unwrinkles' far beyond the confines of the body, in the stars, while the 'secret of the soil' enters (or exits) via the eye. Without unduly confining the poem's complex meanings, we can at least suggest that Thomas is attempting to chart inner processes by reference to external phenomena, and to suggest the interdependence of the two worlds.

I think, however, that most of us will want to go further than this in our attempts to elucidate the poem; while bearing in mind the notion that any 'truth' we discover may be liable to qualification or even subversion by alternative possibilities (Yeats' term 'counter-truth' seems useful in this context), we can nevertheless move towards a more detailed understanding of its complexities.

The inner light of the first stanza isn't precisely located or defined but it seems reasonable, particularly in view of the later reference to dawn's breaking 'behind the eyes', to locate it within the brain. I use the phrase 'within the brain' in order to preserve something of the ambiguity of Thomas' own statement: we may wish to foreground the physiological fact of the brain's recreation, in its own dark recesses, of the light of the outer world, or to give prominence to the idea of psychological or spiritual illumination; but it doesn't seem helpful to reject either reading in favour of the other. The image of the heart, traditionally seen not only as an organ central to the body's physiological functioning but also as the seat of the emotions, perpetuates this ambiguity: the tidal waters undoubtedly represent the pulsing blood, but may also hint at more abstract energies.

Further ambiguities emerge as we read on. What do we make of the word 'file' in the last line of the first stanza? My own reading gives primacy to a vision of the 'things of light' filing, in the sense of processing, through a skeletal structure – the paradoxical 'through the flesh where no flesh decks the bones' permitting a sense of the flesh's absence as well as of its presence; 'tides' has already generated the notion of a submarine world, and these luminous creatures present themselves to my mind in the form of those phosphorescent fish which inhabit the deeper regions of the sea. At the same time, however, I'm aware of a subsidiary suggestion: to 'file through' may imply the rasping away of the flesh, perhaps by the abrasive mouth-parts of those vaguely defined marine creatures. You might feel at first that you need to decide between these two interpretations; on reflection, however, it may strike you that Thomas' insistence on the simultaneous absence and presence of the flesh not only allows you to hold both ideas in mind at once but actually encourages you to do so. You might like to think in this connection, of the significance of the phrase 'When logics die', in the final stanza, bearing in mind Thomas' emphatic suggestion that his poetry does not move 'from one logical point to another'.

We approach this final stanza through a series of images further suggestive of illumination, as well as of procreation. The first line of the stanza half-echoes the poem's opening line, but the light is now defined as breaking 'in secret lots'. 'Secret' again implies inwardness; 'lot' seems here to signify (primarily, if not exclusively) a plot of land, and the fact that this usage is much more widely current in the United States than in Britain may alert you to the possibility that this is a literary borrowing. I'd suggest that Thomas may well be remembering, or half-remembering, T. S. Eliot's 'worlds' which 'revolve like ancient women/Gathering fuel in vacant lots' in the 'Preludes' of 1917. 'Tips' serves to reinforce this possibility, throwing us back to the 'sordid images' of Eliot's sequence, but 'tips of thought' may suggest not only the detritus of the inner world but a delicate outgrowth like that of a plant; both the reference to spring at the end of the preceding stanza and the later line 'The secret of the soil grows through the eye' help to provide a context for such a reading.

What happens 'when logics die'? Thomas' suggestion is, I believe, of a form of liberation, one with implications for his own creative activities: freed from logical restraint, life flourishes, its growth eroding the boundary between inner and outer worlds. It's not simply that the breaching of the eye, the interface of those worlds, effects a link between them; more disturbingly, we are now deeply uncertain of the distinction between the two. Although the 'soil' might well be that of the outer world imaged by the beholder (and I don't think we can reject such a reading) we are also encouraged, by the repetition of 'secret', to visualize growth as originating in the inward 'secret lots' of the stanza's opening line; this reading is reinforced if you accept my interpretation of 'tips of thought' as partially suggestive of organic outgrowth.

A similar uncertainty is likely to underlie our reading of the poem's penultimate line. Has the sun now broken through into those areas where, in the first stanza, 'no sun shines', or has blood been let, so that it now leaps from the body into sunlight? (The notion of wounding or death in the latter case may qualify, but doesn't negate, the affirmative vitality of 'grows' and 'jumps'.) Here as elsewhere, I don't believe that we have to make the choice; on the contrary, it's by accommodating both possibilities that we will most fully appreciate a poem whose final image of perpetual dawn is intimately linked with suggestions of the fruitful fusion of apparently separate worlds.

'Light Breaks Where No Sun Shines' is clearly a difficult poem to analyse, and you may also have been aware, as you examined it, of a difficulty in relating it to most of the poems we've looked at so far: perhaps you registered Thomas' oscillation – by no means uncharacteristic – between a vague evocation of cosmic immensities and a self-centred preoccupation with physical and mental functions, and felt the consequent lack of any significant focus on the broadly social themes central to the poetry of so many of his contemporaries. Certainly Thomas must be seen as atypical (though this begs the question of what a 'typical' poet of the period might be) but I don't believe that we can regard his poetry as irrelevant to our study. To omit a poet of such considerable stature on the grounds that his work doesn't accord with our view of the decade is self-evidently distortive; if that view doesn't accommodate him, it may be that we need to enlarge its scope.

It may be, too, that other poems by Thomas will seem to you to be more readily relatable to the prevalent concerns of the 1930s. 'The Hand That Signed the Paper' (p. 153) has been placed by Skelton in the 'And I Remember Spain' section of the anthology; and although its date precludes any direct association with the Spanish Civil War itself, you'll see immediately that this is a poem dominated by the idea of war. Thomas envisages a conflict initiated by a hand whose signature sets in motion the forces of destruction: the fall of a city is the prelude to the loss of half the inhabitants of a nation, as well as to an act of regicide. The 'sovereign fingers', later characterized as 'these five kings', are portrayed as usurpers of royal prerogatives and, though the subsequent reference to their being 'cramped with chalk' may suggest a certain ignobility, the extent of their power is undeniable.

By portraying the hand as dissociate from the body (the first line of the second stanza sketches in the detail of the 'sloping shoulder' but takes us no further) Thomas is adumbrating the more explicit suggestion of the poem's final stanza: it is detachment which allows the suffering of war to continue. The fingers which 'count the dead' deal only in the statistics of war; their failure to 'soften' (the positioning of the verb at the end of the line encourages us to read it as both transitive and intransitive) represents at once an inability to remedy their own 'cramped' rigidity and a reluctance to heal the wounds they have caused.

I imagine you've found this poem more accessible than 'Light Breaks Where No Sun Shines', but I wonder if you feel, as I do, that it's an inferior work. Its ambiguities seem less richly meaningful and on occasion perhaps unhelpfully confusing: what did you make, for example, of the phrase 'doubled the globe of dead'? There's also a perceptible clumsiness in the delivery of its message: I'm uneasy about the trite irony of 'great is the hand' in the third stanza, and I have some sympathy with G. S. Fraser's suggestion that the poem's concluding line is bathetically inept.[7]

Allan Rodway, distinguishing between the 'social' and the 'personal' poets of the 1930s, places Thomas firmly in the latter category. This seems broadly unexceptionable, but we shouldn't underestimate the significance of the attempt, in 'The Hand That Signed the Paper', to assume a more public role; and we might usefully move on from this observation to examine 'In Memory of Ann Jones' (p. 122), arguably a much more successful poem and one which deals centrally with the idea of the poet as 'bard'. Thomas is clearly giving the term much of its Celtic resonance as he portrays himself standing on a dais (the 'raised hearth' which, for all its localized homeliness, is also a platform from which profound truths may be uttered) giving an oration to the memory of his dead aunt. If this last detail again implies a rather homely variant on the Oxford English Dictionary's definition of the Celtic bard as one who composes verses to celebrate 'the achievements of chiefs and warriors' and to enshrine 'historical and traditional facts', this shouldn't be seen as negating the powerful suggestion that Thomas, as poet, is addressing himself to an essentially public task.

Thomas is himself aware, of course, of the discrepancy between traditional bardic utterance and his own mundane circumstances. Standing in a room with 'a stuffed fox and a stale fern', the inert debris of a low-key life, he graduates to the elevated diction and imagery of 'Whose hooded, fountain heart once fell in puddles/Round the parched worlds of Wales and drowned each sun', only to check himself with the observation that the image is disproportionate to the fact; the idea of a revivifying (though also obliterating) abundance of water is expressly qualified by that of Ann's death as a 'still drop'. It's clear, however, that the celebratory impulse persists: the succeeding image of the 'holy/Flood' throws us back to the earlier fall of water on 'parched worlds' and paves the way for a reassertion of Ann's right, however modest her wishes, to the poet's ritualistic eloquence.

It's not just the poet's own eloquence which is suggested here: his 'call' is for a complementary eloquence in the world around him; and the notion of the rigid inexpressiveness of a 'wood-tongued virtue' being transformed into babbling loquacity (not, I think, a negative idea in this context) is reinforced by the subsequent references to the 'hymning heads' and a love which 'sings' through the chapel. Thomas' consciousness of stark actuality then surfaces again in a passage suggestive of shabbiness and confinement, but the circumscription implicit in such words as 'humble', 'cramp', 'threadbare' and 'clenched' is dramatically challenged by the poem's concluding lines which, hinting at the eternal ('forever'), offer a vision of transcendence. The stuffed fox and the stale fern, formerly emblems of death and degeneration, now realign themselves with the forces of life, the vigorously procreative plant perhaps taking its cue from the isolated but potent word uttered by the fox's twitching lung.

If you agree with me that this is a poem dominated by the concept of verbal utterance, and take my point about the poet's insistence on his own bardic role, you may find yourself disinclined to separate Thomas too neatly from his more obviously 'social' contemporaries. This response might be strengthened by consideration of Thomas' increasingly public profile during the following decade and beyond: like Louis MacNeice, he was to exploit the medium of radio with considerable skill; and the poetry readings of his last three years, while undeniably reflecting his perpetual need for money, also bear testimony to his sense of the poet's organic relationship to the society he serves.

8. Evaluations

Well before the close of the decade, the poets of the 1930s were offering critical evaluations of one another's work; I've already given passing mention to the most important of these. C. Day Lewis' *A Hope for Poetry* appeared as early as 1934 and, while not exclusively devoted to the poets of its author's generation, gave those poets considerable prominence; it also tended to reinforce the notion of a group identity. It's possible to take a rather cynical view of Day Lewis' repeated reference to his own verse, and of his linking of that verse with the work of more talented contemporaries; but he certainly recognized many of the trends of the decade's poetry, and touches usefully on such matters as the relationship between psychology and poetry, the interplay of public and private meaning and the assimilation, by poets, of material formerly regarded as inappropriate to poetry. It's not a deeply thoughtful or coherent study, but does give insight into the mind of a young writer eager to articulate his perceptions of a creative ferment in which he is himself embroiled.

Stephen Spender's *The Destructive Element*, published in

the following year, deals in its six final chapters with the vexed question of literature's relationship to politics. Spender gives some space to Day Lewis' poetry, but his fuller sympathy with Auden's work is expressed in a concluding chapter which addresses a number of early poems, as well as *The Orators* and the verse-play *The Dance of Death*. For Spender, one of Auden's chief strengths is his accommodating love of the world:

> His gift is the peculiar gift of a writer who does not write from rejecting his experiences, nor from strict selection among many appearances, but accepting more and more of life and of ideas as he goes on experiencing.[1]

This is perceptive, if grammatically lax, criticism: Spender's vision of a poetry informed by multiple perspectives helps to explain both that poetry's variegated richness and its lack of an identifiable ideological centre.

In the first chapter of his discursive and engaging *Modern Poetry* (1938), Louis MacNeice quotes from Michael Roberts' 1932 preface to *New Signatures* before going on to offer his own similarly generalized account of 'these new poets'.[2] Like Roberts' generalizations, MacNeice's are sometimes questionable, but his knowledge of the poetry of his immediate contemporaries is undeniably impressive. Auden features particularly prominently, MacNeice quoting extensively from his early work; but the principal value of the study, significantly subtitled 'A Personal Essay', lies in what MacNeice tells us about himself and about his own poetic attitudes and practice.

I want us to turn now to studies of the 1930s published after the end of the decade, in order to see how later criticism attempted retrospectively to define this complex period and the diverse body of poetry it produced. Writing in 1941, Francis Scarfe, himself a poet whose verse can be found in Skelton's anthology, was clearly not inclined to isolate the preceding decade: his study, *Auden and After*, is subtitled 'The Liberation of Poetry 1930–1941', the suggestion being that neither the outbreak of war nor the conclusion of the decade itself has brought to a close the minor poetic revolution he identifies; it might also be noted that, while the title suggests that the publication of Auden's *Poems* in 1930 is the seminal event, Scarfe's introduction takes us back to 1929 and the publication of Day Lewis' *Transitional Poem*.

Like Michael Roberts nearly a decade earlier, Scarfe defines his group of poets in generational terms: all are members of ' "The War Generation" (the children of the last war and the conscripts of this)'.[3] But he rightly insists on their individuality as writers,

and complicates the picture by identifying four sub-groups within
the poetic generation:

> the Auden group which includes Spender, [Day] Lewis and MacNeice;
> the 'New Verse' group led by Grigson, and which was closely identi-
> fied with the Auden group; the 'Twentieth Century Verse' group
> under Julian Symons . . . and, finally, a rather heterogeneous group
> of sensualists, mystics and romantic extremists ranging from Dylan
> Thomas to the neo-Surrealists and the Apocalypse.[4]

You'll notice that Scarfe's categories are breaking down even as he
attempts to establish them: the *New Verse* group is acknowledged
to be 'closely identified with' the Auden group, while the fourth
group is defined as 'heterogeneous'; and Scarfe goes on to refer
explicitly to the difficulty of categorization in this general context.
Auden and After has long been out of print but is worth a glance
if you can get hold of a copy. Its critical stance, such as it is, lacks
sophistication, but the study represents a preliminary mapping out
of the terrain to be covered more effectively by later critics.

The first major retrospective study of the period's poetry
appeared in 1969. D. E. S. Maxwell's *Poets of the Thirties* begins
with a chapter which, as we've already noted, seeks to define the
poetry largely in relation to its historical context; entitled 'Marx
and the Muse', it's a chapter which also emphasizes the political
orientation of the poets, sometimes misleadingly. Take this passage,
for example, in which Maxwell, having accurately observed that
Marxist vocabulary 'made it possible to talk of hair-raising violence without having to visualise the reality', yokes together in
support of his pronouncement two phrases from a poem we've
already looked at – Day Lewis' *The Magnetic Mountain* 25 – and
two from Auden's early work:

> Contemporary left-wing poetry . . . disguised the messiness of actually
> killing people. Surgery provided a convenient image: 'The hour of
> the knife', 'the major operation', 'a bed, hard, surgical/And a wound
> hurting', the 'surgeon's idea of pain'.[5]

We haven't looked at the two poems by Auden in which the last
two phrases appear; but you might like to ask yourself whether
Day Lewis' naive and rather callous enthusiasm, undoubtedly
germane to Maxwell's argument, is likely to find a direct parallel
in the more complex and sophisticated poetry of Auden. The
phrase 'surgeon's idea of pain' actually comes from a poem which
appeared in *New Country* in 1933 as 'Prologue'; let's look at its
immediate context:

> Some dream, say yes, long coiled in the ammonite's slumber
> Is uncurling, prepared to lay on our talk and kindness
> Its military silence, its surgeon's idea of pain.

The lines are actually ambiguous, permitting Maxwell's reading of them as 'left-wing poetry', but seeming to offer a much broader range of meaning, while the poet's attitude to the development he describes seems inescapably ambivalent. Do you feel that the lines are evasive in the way suggested? Or is Maxwell misrepresenting Auden?

You may want to reflect further on that question when we've examined the preceding quotation in context; the bed and wound appear in the following stanza from the first of the 'Six Odes' in *The Orators*:

> Shaped me a Lent scene first, a bed, hard, surgical
>   And a wound hurting;
> The hour in the night when Lawrence died and I came
>   Round from the morphia.
> A train went clanking over the bridges leaving the city;
> A sleep-walker pushed on groaning down the velvet passage;
> The night-nurse visited – 'We shall not all sleep, dearie',
>   She said, and left me.

Is this an example of a poet disguising the messiness of political murder through the use of surgical imagery? Even without having separate access to the biographical information that the poem refers to an operation undergone by Auden shortly before its composition, the intelligent reader is unlikely to endorse Maxwell's view.

I've spent some time on these details because they bring to the fore certain issues which I regard as crucial to this chapter. It's one of the roles of the critic to order the text or texts under review into a reasonably coherent pattern; in the case of the poetry of the 1930s – a massive and diverse body of texts from a muddled and volatile period of history – such patterning may seem particularly desirable while at the same time proving especially difficult. Maxwell is a perceptive critic, and his study is generally a good one; but he has here betrayed the text, dragging it into the service of his critical model, rather than using that model in the service of the text. This is a recurrent problem in literary criticism, and the reader's best safeguard is to keep an eye firmly on the text, constantly testing the critic's statements and theories against the actual words of the author.

Maxwell's primary interest in the political orientation of his chosen poets helps to explain the otherwise slightly puzzling balance of his study: more space is devoted to the minor Communist poets Christopher Caudwell and John Cornford ('Poets in the Party') than to MacNeice and Spender, while Day Lewis is accorded vastly more attention than any other poet represented, with the exception of Auden. Maxwell's criteria are not, fundamentally, aesthetic ones; his is one of a number of valid approaches, but we need, as in the case of all criticism, to remain aware of the study's particular bias.

A. T. Tolley's *The Poetry of the Thirties* (1975) is a less tendentious work, based on the author's awareness that 'the appearance of a dominating concern with political themes'[6] is inadequate as a means of defining the poetry of the decade, and providing a somewhat fragmented vision of a period explicitly represented as less homogeneous than it appears in popular memory. There is, certainly, a chapter entitled 'Poetry and Politics', and suggestions of a relationship between the two are recurrent throughout the volume; but the attention given to such poets as David Gascoyne, Kathleen Raine and Julian Symons confirms Tolley's determination not to be confined by stereotypic views of his subject. You'll find useful guidance here, but you may also register a certain dullness about the survey, which seems not to engage fully with any of the wide range of topics upon which it touches.

Published in 1976, Samuel Hynes' *The Auden Generation* still seems to me to stand as one of the best accounts of the 1930s. Subtitled 'Literature and Politics in England in the 1930s', it addresses the prose of the decade as well as the poetry and, by adopting a chronological approach, manages to impose a kind of order on its immense subject while at the same time suggesting the significant shifts of outlook and emphasis which took place over the period as a whole. Like Maxwell, Hynes promotes a historicist vision, asserting from the outset that he does not believe 'that literary history can be separated from social and political and economic history'.[7] Nevertheless, he is careful to add, 'the subject [of the study] is literature'.

Hynes' understanding of history is acute and subtle and he posits a distinction, universally applicable but particularly relevant to the 1930s, between history itself, uncertain and confusing, and the myths which solidify out of the original flux. 'In studying the past', he argues, 'we must try by an act of the imagination to recover that sense of fluidity'.[8] How do you respond to this suggestion? Isn't it easier to work with the more solid images and ideas provided by distance and hindsight? And can we, in any case, hope to recover the authentic flavour of a past to which we no longer belong, or have never belonged? You may wish to acknowledge both the value and the inevitability of some degree of detachment from the past, yet to register at the same time the desirability of that imaginative reappropriation of which Hynes speaks.

Bernard Bergonzi's *Reading the Thirties* (1978) also tackles the subject on a relatively broad front. You may be a little puzzled by the unnecessarily defensive introduction, in which Bergonzi argues for the novelty of his own approach: 'My interest', he asserts, clearly with the intention of effecting a partial dissociation of his own work from that of his predecessors in the field, 'is less in discussing individual authors, or individual texts, than in trying to read the thirties as a collective subject, even as a collective text'.[9] In arguing his case, Bergonzi claims relationship with Continental rather than Anglo-American critical models; yet the truth is that, from the publication of *New Signatures* in 1932, the idea of the 1930s as a collective text has been a dominant feature of most literary accounts of the period. Bergonzi rightly points out that the shared experiences of class privilege and, peripherally, of the First World War may have been more significant than any presumed left-wing sympathies; but his insistence on the inclusion of 'writers who were apolitical or right-wing' had already been pre-empted by Hynes, whose excellent account of Evelyn Waugh's *Vile Bodies* – 'a generation-defining work', as Hynes significantly characterizes it – forms an entire sub-section of his study's second chapter. It might be added that Hynes' similarly extensive account of Graham Greene's *It's a Battlefield* functions as an implicit corrective to Bergonzi's remarkable inclusion of Greene in the 'apolitical or right-wing' category.

Where Bergonzi seems to me to be stronger is in his following through of his argument for a more flexible approach to the totality of cultural experience. Acknowledging the influence of the Structuralist philosopher Roland Barthes, he urges the adoption of a model in which the idea of literature and its background as related but ultimately distinct entities is replaced by a vision of interpenetrative fields of force; the very concepts of 'background' and 'foreground' become, in the light of such a vision, difficult to sustain. The image on the dust-wrapper of the book is in every sense provocative: not one of the poets or novelists of the 1930s, but one of the great cinematic icons of the period, Greta Garbo; and Bergonzi moves freely and illuminatingly, in the course of his study, across a broad cultural field, noting the affinities between MacNeice's poetry and the lyrics of Ira Gershwin or picking up on Waugh's implied distaste for the kind of architectural innovation associated with Walter Gropius and the Bauhaus school of design in Germany.

Valentine Cunningham, whose monumental *British Writers of the Thirties* appeared in 1988, adopts a similar approach to his material: 'This book', he asserts in his opening chapter, 'does not propose to endorse the separations between "literature" on the one hand and "society" on the other that are still all too conventional in literary historical discussions.'[10] As if to affirm his own credentials, he at once identifies the flaw in his immediate predecessor's argument: Bergonzi's talk of texts and contexts, Cunningham points out, actually confirms the divisive vision. The point is valid, though you may feel uneasy about Cunningham's failure to acknowledge the extent to which Bergonzi's arguments *do* work against the artificial separation of literature and society.

Cunningham's study amasses an extraordinary amount of material from the 1930s, drawing extensively on sources more or less ignored by previous critics, to create a much fuller picture than any to date. You may sense, however, that there's a lack of incisiveness about the study, a tendency to anthologize rather than to develop critical argument. The point throws us back to our earlier discussion: Maxwell's tendentious and highly selective approach lies at the opposite extreme to this sprawling acknowledgement of the richness and diversity of a decade.

Michael O'Neill and Gareth Reeves' *Auden, MacNeice, Spender: The Thirties Poetry* (1992) is more correctly understood as an account of the work of three thirties poets than as a survey of the decade's poetry as a whole. Studies of individual poets lie beyond the scope of this chapter (though a select list of such works will be found among my 'Suggestions for Further Reading' at the end of the book) but this study, focused on the relevant period and dealing interconnectedly with its three most significant poets, clearly demands acknowledgement here.

O'Neill and Reeves explicitly differentiate their approach from that of Cunningham, acknowledging the strengths of their predecessor's integrative vision, but insisting on the value of the aesthetic response – a response which in my view has played too small a part in critical evaluation of the literature of the 1930s – and quoting Helen Vendler's valuable dictum that 'aesthetic criticism begins with the effort to understand the individual work'.[11] The study certainly contributes to our general understanding of the period; but its broader perspectives are dependent upon its analytical readings of individual texts. My personal belief that such generalizations as we allow ourselves must be approached via the specific is very largely mirrored in O'Neill and Reeves' study; this is the survey whose basic approach most closely resembles my own.

It isn't, of course, my role to tell you what critical approach you yourself should adopt in getting to grips with the literature of this or any other period. In reading the work of critics you're likely to find some models particularly helpful or congenial, and these will inevitably influence your thinking; but you would be unwise to regard any model as definitive. Remain alert to the deficiencies, as well as the strengths, of your preferred critics; and bear in mind my earlier advice to test their accounts repeatedly against the literary texts themselves. If those texts seem to you to provide something beyond, or even radically different from, the account you've been offered, don't hesitate to investigate further; literary criticism is too important a matter to be left to the specialists.

It might be helpful if, as we bring our discussion to a close, you were to draw together your current impressions of the poetry of the 1930s. What patterns and affinities can you now distinguish? Have you been obliged, as a result of our readings, to jettison any of the views you previously held? What views have taken their place? Has our close analysis revealed genuine literary strengths, or do you find the poetry merely or primarily of historical and social interest? What significant areas seem to you to have been left unexplored by our necessarily incomplete survey?

These are questions which will require considerable thought. Some of your answers are likely to be complex and will, moreover, be subject to revision as your acquaintance with the poetry grows. For the conclusion of this guide shouldn't be regarded as the end of your explorations: my purpose has been to chart the salient features of this difficult and rewarding area of study; your task now is to continue the process of discovery.

Notes

Chapter 1 – Definitions

1 Dobrée, 'New Life in English Poetry', *The Listener*, IX, No. 231 (14 June 1933), p. 958.
2 Grigson, 'Faith or Feeling?', *New Verse*, 2 (March 1933).
3 Grigson, *A Skull in Salop* (Macmillan, 1967).
4 Maxwell, *Poets of the Thirties*, p. 1.
5 Roberts, *Critique of Poetry* (Cape, 1934), p. 238.
6 Larkin, 'MCMXIV', *The Whitsun Weddings* (Faber, 1964).
7 Hynes, *The Auden Generation*, p. 17.
8 Lehmann, *The Whispering Gallery* (Longmans, 1955), p. 138.
9 MacNeice, 'Aubade', *Collected Poems*.
10 Bell, 'Marsh Birds Pass Over London', *Winter Movement*, (Chatto and Windus, 1930).
11 Auden, *The Orators*; in *The English Auden*, p. 62.
12 Lehmann, *The Whispering Gallery*, p. 217.
13 MacNeice, *Autumn Journal*; in *Collected Poems*.
14 Karl Marx and Friedrich Engels, *The Communist Manifesto*; translation by Eden and Cedar Paul (Martin Lawrence, 1930), p. 38.
15 Bell, Letter to Jane Simone Bussy, 26 April 1936. In *Julian Bell: Essays, Poems and Letters* (Hogarth, 1938), p. 111.
16 Roberts, preface to *New Country* (Hogarth, 1933), pp. 9–10.
17 Sigmund Freud, *The Ego and the Id*, Standard Edition, vol. XIX (Hogarth, 1961), p. 23.
18 Freud, *Introductory Lectures on Psycho-Analysis*, Standard Edition, vol. XV (Hogarth, 1963), p. 49.
19 Bradbury and McFarlane, *Modernism 1890–1930* (Penguin, 1976), p. 52.
20 Ibid., p. 48.
21 Spender, *World Within World*, p. 59.
22 Skelton, *Poetry of the Thirties*, p. 27.
23 MacNeice, *The Poetry of W. B. Yeats* (Oxford, 1941), p. 41.
24 Grigson, review in *New Verse*, 6 (December 1933).
25 Allott, *New Verse*, New Series, I, No. 2 (May 1939).
26 MacNeice, *The Poetry of W. B. Yeats*, p. 1.

Chapter 2 – Setting the Tone: W. H. Auden

1 Symons, *The Thirties*, p. 14.
2 Lehmann, *The Whispering Gallery*, p. 175.
3 Grigson, 'The Reason for This', *New Verse*, No. 26/27 (November 1937).
4 Grigson, 'W. H. Auden', *Times Literary Supplement* (5 October 1973).
5 Spender, *World Within World*, pp. 51–2.
6 Quoted in Mendelson, *Early Auden* (Faber, 1981), p. 46.
7 Isherwood, *Lions and Shadows* (Hogarth, 1938), p. 302.
8 Auden, Foreword to *Collected Shorter Poems* (Faber, 1966).
9 Thomas, *New Verse*, 26/27 (November 1937).
10 Mendelson, *Early Auden*, p. 143.
11 Ibid., p. 144.
12 Cunningham, in K. Bucknell and N. Jenkins (eds), *The Map of All My Youth* (Clarendon, 1990), p. 184.
13 Auden, *The Orators*, 3rd edn, p. 7.
14 Auden (with John Garrett), *The Poet's Tongue* (Bell, 1935), p. ix.
15 Allan Rodway, *Poetry of the 1930s* (Longmans, 1967), p. 13.
16 Orwell, 'Inside the Whale', *Collected Essays, Journalism and Letters*, Vol. 1 (Penguin, 1970), p. 566.
17 Slater, 'The Turning Point', *Left Review*, 2, No. 1 (October 1935).
18 Auden and Garrett, *The Poet's Tongue*, p. vi.
19 Auden, *Poets of the English Language* (Eyre and Spottiswoode, 1952), p. xxx.
20 Thucydides, *History of the Peloponnesian War*, translated by Rex Warner (Penguin, 1970), p. 213.
21 Ibid., p. 48.
22 Foreword, B. C. Bloomfield, *W. H. Auden: A Bibliography* (University of Virginia, 1964), p. viii.
23 Auden, letter written, but not sent, to Naomi Mitchison in 1967; quoted in Mendelson, *Early Auden*, p. 330.
24 Mendelson, *Early Auden*, pp. 326–8.
25 Edward Callan, *Auden: A Carnival of Intellect* (Oxford, 1983), p. 156.

Chapter 3 – A Window on the World: Stephen Spender

1 Hulme, *Speculations* (Routledge and Kegan Paul, 2nd edn, 1936), p. 109.
2 See Cunningham, *British Writers of the Thirties*, p. 154.
3 Spender, 'Poetry and Revolution', *New Country*, p. 62.
4 Day Lewis, *A Hope for Poetry* (Basil Blackwell, 1934), p. 2.
5 Spender, *The Thirties and After* (Fontana, 1978), p. 18.
6 Ibid., p. 18.
7 Spender, *World Within World*, p. 233.
8 Spender, *The Destructive Element* (Cape, 1935), p. 256.
9 Ibid., p. 13.
10 Roberts, preface to *New Country*, p. 19.

Chapter 4 – A Sense of Loss: Louis MacNeice

1 MacNeice, *The Strings are False*, p. 37.
2 Ibid., p. 37.
3 MacNeice, *Modern Poetry* (Oxford, 2nd edn, 1968), p. 134.
4 MacNeice, *The Strings are False*, p. 133.

Chapter 5 – Between Two Fires: C. Day Lewis

1 Day Lewis, *The Buried Day*, p. 213.
2 Ibid., pp. 223, 225.
3 Ibid., p. 213.
4 Day Lewis, 'Letter to a Young Revolutionary', *New Country*, pp. 30–1.
5 Day Lewis, *The Buried Day*, p. 213.
6 Ibid., p. 209.
7 Wyndham Lewis, *Men Without Art* (Cassell, 1934), p. 273.
8 Bell, *Essays, Poems and Letters*, p. 309.
9 A. J. P. Taylor, *English History 1914–1945* (Oxford, 1965), p. 313.
10 Ibid., p. 181.
11 Ibid., p. 181.

Chapter 6 – Observations: Geoffrey Grigson, Bernard Spencer, Kenneth Allott

1 Grigson, 'Lonely, But Not Lonely Enough', *New Verse*, 31/32 (Autumn 1938).
2 Grigson, *The Crest on the Silver*, p. 170.
3 Allott, 'Several Things', *New Verse*, 31/32 (Autumn 1938).
4 Roy Fuller, 'Poems by Editors', *Twentieth Century Verse*, 17 (April–May 1939).
5 Martin Dodsworth, 'Bernard Spencer: The Poet of Addition', *The Review*, 11/12.
6 MacNeice, *Modern Poetry*, p. 107.
7 Allott, 'David Gascoyne', *Programme*, 16 (6 May 1936).

Chapter 7 – Inner and Outer Worlds: David Gascoyne, Dylan Thomas

1 André Breton, 'Limits not Frontiers of Surrealism', in *Surrealism*, ed. Herbert Read (Faber, 1936), p. 102.
2 Quoted by Gascoyne in *A Short Survey of Surrealism* (Cobden-Sanderson, 1935), p. 61.
3 Gascoyne, *New Verse*, 11 (October 1934).
4 Lehmann, *The Noise of History* (Hogarth, 1934).
5 Paul Ferris, *Dylan Thomas*, (Penguin, 1978), p. 6.
6 Ferris (ed.), *Dylan Thomas: The Collected Letters* (Dent, 1985), p. 281.
7 G. S. Fraser, *Dylan Thomas* (Longmans, Green and Co., 1957), p. 14.

Chapter 8 – Evaluations

1 Spender, *The Destructive Element*, p. 276.
2 MacNeice, *Modern Poetry*, p. 15.
3 Scarfe, *Auden and After*, p. viii.
4 Ibid., p. ix.
5 Maxwell, *Poets of the Thirties*, p. 4.
6 Tolley, *The Poetry of the Thirties*, p. 11.
7 Hynes, *The Auden Generation*, p. 9.
8 Ibid., p. 12.
9 Bergonzi, *Reading the Thirties*, p. 2.
10 Cunningham, *British Writers of the Thirties*, p. 1.
11 O'Neill and Reeves, *Auden, MacNeice, Spender: The Thirties Poetry*, p. 1.

Suggestions for Further Reading

Our survey of the poetry of the 1930s has necessarily been selective, and my first recommendation is that you embark, if you haven't already done so, on a wider reading of Skelton's anthology; there are other strong and distinctive voices represented here, including those of George Barker, Norman Cameron and William Empson. Beyond this, I'd suggest a fuller examination of the work of those poets discussed in the present survey.

   The English Auden (Faber, 1977), edited by Edward Mendelson, collects together Auden's thirties poetry, along with the essays and some of the dramatic writings of the period. The poetry appears here in the form in which it was published during the decade itself. This is an important point; Auden's significant later revisions make the *Collected Shorter Poems* of 1966 largely untrustworthy from our point of view. If you can't get hold of *The English Auden*, the *Selected Poems* of 1979 (Faber), also edited by Mendelson, is a good substitute: more than a third of the selection is accounted for by poems written during the 1930s, again published in the form in which they appeared at the time.

   Day Lewis' unwillingness to 'reconstruct' earlier poems means that his *Collected Poems* of 1954 (Jonathan Cape) offers an accurate, if slightly abbreviated, record of his thirties output; the omissions from that volume have been restored in the *Complete Poems* of 1992 (Sinclair-Stevenson). MacNeice's determination to keep revisions to a minimum has ensured that the *Collected Poems* of 1949 and its successor of 1966 (both Faber) are also essentially reliable. The publication of Spender's 1955 *Collected Poems* (Faber) was, however, the occasion for a number of 'improvements' (Spender's own term) while the 1985 edition involved further revision. In neither case do the revisions radically alter individual poems, but the original collections from the 1930s – *Poems* (Faber, 1933) and *The Still Centre* (Faber, 1939) – represent a more reliable source, and you may be able to track these down.

   Geoffrey Grigson also revised for his *Collected Poems* (Phoenix House, 1963) but the rarity of his only thirties collection, *Several Observations* (Cresset, 1939) means that the later collected edition may have to suffice. David Gascoyne's *Collected Poems* of 1965 (Oxford) omitted a surprising amount of thirties material, but the revised edition of 1988 provides a fuller picture of Gascoyne's work during the decade.

Kenneth Allott's *Collected Poems* was published in 1975 by Secker and Warburg, with a foreword by Roy Fuller. Bernard Spencer also had his poems posthumously collected, once in 1965 (Alan Ross) and again, in a more scholarly edition, in 1981 (Oxford University Press) with an introduction and notes by Roger Bowen. Dylan Thomas' *Collected Poems* can also be found in two editions, that of 1952 and the usefully annotated edition of 1988, a volume claimed by its editors, Walford Davies and Ralph Maud, to be 'as definitive as present scholarship allows'.

Literary biographies and autobiographies often prove illuminating. I've mentioned a number of such works in the course of the survey, and you might find it helpful to be provided with a select list as an aid to further exploration:

C. Day Lewis, *The Buried Day* (Chatto and Windus, 1960).
Paul Ferris, *Dylan Thomas* (Hodder and Stoughton, 1977; Penguin Books, 1978).
Geoffrey Grigson, *The Crest on the Silver* (Cresset, 1950).
Louis MacNeice, *The Strings are False* (Faber, 1965).
Edward Mendelson, *Early Auden* (Faber, 1981).
Stephen Spender, *World Within World* (Hamish Hamilton, 1951).

Letters and journals of the period have also been published: you'll find relevant material in the early parts of Stephen Spender's *Journals 1939–1983* (Faber, 1985) and Dylan Thomas' *Collected Letters* (Dent, 1985) as well as in David Gascoyne's *Journals* (Enitharmon Press, 1978 and 1980).

You might also like to have listed here the major studies of the decade's poetry. We discussed these briefly in Chapter 8, but all will repay further attention:

Bernard Bergonzi, *Reading the Thirties* (Macmillan, 1978).
Valentine Cunningham, *British Writers of the Thirties* (Oxford, 1988).
Samuel Hynes, *The Auden Generation* (Bodley Head, 1976).
D. E. S. Maxwell, *Poets of the Thirties* (Routledge, 1969).
Michael O'Neill and Gareth Reeves, *Auden, MacNeice, Spender: The Thirties Poetry* (Macmillan, 1992).
Francis Scarfe, *Auden and After* (Routledge, 1942).
A. T. Tolley, *The Poetry of the Thirties* (Gollancz, 1975).

Julian Symons' cultural history, *The Thirties: A Dream Revolved* (revised edition, Faber, 1975) provides interesting background material.

Finally, there are a number of studies dealing individually with the most widely known of the poets of the 1930s. Auden has received a considerable amount of critical attention, and your reading in this area is likely to be, of necessity, highly selective. Among works you're likely to find particularly helpful and relevant are Frederick Buell's *Auden as a Social Poet* (Cornell University Press, 1973); Edward Callan's *Auden: A Carnival of Intellect* (Oxford, 1983); John Fuller's *A Reader's Guide to W. H. Auden* (Thames and Hudson, 1970); Justin Replogle's *Auden's Poetry* (Methuen, 1969); Stan Smith's *Auden* (Blackwell, 1985); and Monroe K. Spears' *The Poetry of W. H. Auden* (Oxford, 1963).

Louis MacNeice is the subject of William T. McKinnon's *Apollo's Blended Dream* (Oxford, 1971) and of Robyn Marsack's *The Cave of Making* (Clarendon, 1982). Edna Longley's *Louis MacNeice: A Study* (Faber, 1988) and Peter McDonald's *Louis MacNeice: The Poet in his Contexts* (Clarendon, 1991) both offer extensive accounts of MacNeice's early work.

Day Lewis and Spender have received far less individual attention, but you'll find useful material in Joseph N. Riddel's *C. Day Lewis* (Twayne, 1971); while Spender figures centrally in A. Kingsley Weatherhead's *Stephen Spender and the Thirties* (Associated University Presses, 1975), a study which also deals in some detail with the work of other poets of the period.

Index